THE CARS THAT
HENRY
FORD
BUILT

*A 75th Anniversary Tribute
to America's Most
Remembered Automobiles*

Book Trade Distribution by E.P. Dutton
2 Park Avenue, New York, New York 10016

AN AUTOMOBILE QUARTERLY LIBRARY SERIES BOOK

THE CARS THAT
HENRY FORD BUILT

*A 75th Anniversary Tribute
to America's
Most Remembered Automobiles*

BY BEVERLY RAE KIMES

AN AUTOMOBILE QUARTERLY LIBRARY SERIES BOOK

Automobile Quarterly Publications

Publisher and President: L. Scott Bailey

Editor: Beverly Rae Kimes

Senior Editor: Stan Grayson

Art Director: Theodore R.F. Hall

Associate Art Director: Kenneth N. Drasser

Editorial Assistant: Eleanor Mueller

Business Manager: Kevin Bitz

The chapters in this book first appeared as a series of articles in AUTOMOBILE *Quarterly* magazine, in the editions following, and copyrighted by Automobile Quarterly, Inc.: "Young Henry Ford," Volume X, Number 2, copyright © 1972; "Henry's Model T," Volume X, Number 4, copyright © 1972; "How Do You Follow A Legend? With Another Legend, Of Course!," Volume XI, Number 4, copyright © 1973; "The Ford Nobody Noticed" and "Last Act: The V-8 Years of Henry Ford," Volume XII, Number 3, copyright © 1974.

Typesetting and printing by Kutztown Publishing Company, Kutztown, Pennsylvania; color separations by Litho-Art, Inc., New York City, Infinity Color Company, Ltd., North Bellemore, New York and Graphic Arts Corporation, Toledo, Ohio; binding by National Publishing Company, Philadelphia, Pennsylvania.

Published simultaneously in Canada by Clarke, Irwin & Company, Limited, Toronto and Vancouver

Library of Congress Catalog Number: 78-51029

ISBN 0-525-0766-3: E.P. Dutton   ISBN 0-915038-08-0: Princeton Publishing Inc.

A number of years ago someone with a devilish wit and a canny knack for wielding dubious statistics suggested that the history of recent publishing proved three subjects to predominate in acceptance potential: biographies of Abraham Lincoln, books revolving around the medical profession and stories about dogs. And the conclusion drawn from these facts? A volume on the subject of Lincoln's doctor's dog couldn't miss being a best-seller.

Some of that same logic might attach itself to the subject of Henry Ford. Certainly no single individual in the history of the automobile has enjoyed—or suffered—such extensive biographical evaluation. The amount of literature on Ford is staggering. It always has been. During his lifetime, rarely did a month pass when he was not the subject of articles as various as the periodicals in which they appeared, and during his era of incredible dominance of the industry, rarely was there a year in which a book did not issue forth with an appraisal of some sort of the Ford phenomenon. It is certainly a measure of the man that accounts of him contemporary to the years of his life tended to be at extremes: either adulatory to the point of embarrassment, or scathing to the extent of being—at the very least—unseemly.

Since his death, with the fortuitous circumstance of retrospect afforded historians for a fresh examination of the man who, simply and clearly, wrought a social revolution, the point of view has changed to the scholarly and objective. The pioneering work begun by Prof. Allan Nevins of Columbia University (in collaboration with Frank Ernest Hill) which resulted in the monumental three-volume history of Ford and which was published beginning in the Fifties, has been followed in the Seventies by the extensive researches and detailed examinations of the man by Prof. David L. Lewis of the University of Michigan. Henry Ford shall probably ever remain a controversial figure. In more recent decades, fortunately, he has come to be viewed as neither godlike

nor satanic, but simply as one quite extraordinary human being.

It was this larger-than-life quality of the Henry Ford persona which initially attracted me. What a compelling, poly-sided man. What a marvelous subject about whom to write. But how? The answer came as I gradually became better acquainted with his cars. How like Henry they were through the years. This is not in itself unusual, a strong personality always places his individual imprint on the object of his creation. But in Henry Ford's case, it was both the duration of his automotive career and a relationship between himself and his cars bordering on the incestuous which holds the intriguing appeal. For the total of his life with the automobile, Henry Ford probably mirrored his cars more accurately than did any other single individual in the history of the industry. And vice versa. His cars were Henry. It is fascinating to watch him grow and age, as his cars grew and aged—as they changed or didn't, as he changed or didn't, each practically in military step with the other.

This then is a study of Henry Ford placed in the context of the cars he built and the environment both within and without the company in which they were produced. The book is divided by section into the various eras of Henry's cars: the divers racing and production machines which preceded the Model T; the revolution-spawning Model T; the interlude of the Model A; the Model B, practically forgotten today and in the early Thirties as well, frequently by Henry himself; and Henry's last act, the Ford V-8.

I like Henry Ford. I like his cars. Though objectivity has been sought throughout, it must be admitted that the portrait herein of Henry Ford is a sympathetic one. And, equally, the presentation of his cars —all in full color—speaks plainly enough of the regard held for them. This book, then, is a tribute to the man and what he created.

PREFACE

Originally the text appeared in a series of articles in
AUTOMOBILE Quarterly magazine. During the course of editing and revising
the stories for this volume, a fresh thought emerged. As intricately
linked as Henry Ford was with his cars, equally entwined
have been the lives of many automobile enthusiasts. Doubtless there are
legions of collectors today whose interest in or acquisition of
historic cars was begun via the Model T, or perhaps the Model A.
Certainly there are more clubs devoted to Ford than to any other individual
marque—and this, it would not be untoward to say, is not
simply for reasons of the cars' ubiquity, but their appeal as well.
And the Ford enthusiast ranks are still being swelled, and often from
unexpected quarters. I've a friend who has an impressive
collection of exotic and sophisticated European machinery of the classic era.
A year or so ago he bought a V-8 Ford of mid-Thirties vintage.
He hasn't stopped talking about it yet. He loves it.

Is there perhaps a devoted automobile enthusiast anywhere in
America who has not had a Ford experience? I've no statistics but I would
tend to think not. I asked another enthusiast friend during the
preparation of this book about it, and the Ford stories fell from his
lips in cascades. Since I had known this gentleman for better than a decade
—as both employee and colleague—I was quite amazed;
I hadn't been aware how Ford cars had paced the formative years of his
automobile enthusiasm. So I asked Scott Bailey—actually I pleaded with him,
he dislikes writing about himself—to share his experiences
in an introduction to this book. I think many people will read it with a
happy feeling of déjà vu and ah-yes-it-was-like-that memories of their own.
I'm most grateful to Scott.

And I owe enormous appreciation to three other friends too.
To Leslie R. Henry, recently retired as curator of the Land Transportation
Section of the Henry Ford Museum and Greenfield Village.

Les knows Ford automobiles as well as most of us do the alphabet,
and his advice and counsel during the writing of the various sections of
this book provided the sort of assurance every writer longs to have.
To Henry Austin Clark, Jr., noted enthusiast, historian and
museum owner, thanks too; as AUTOMOBILE Quarterly's chief of research,
Austin was ever on call to search out an elusive fact or
provide a good and useful sidelight. And gratitude to James J. Bradley,
curator of the National Automotive History Collection
of the Detroit Public Library, whose holdings are a treasure trove,
his gracious allowing of access to which always provides
a spirited treasure hunt with lots of historical surprises.

Appreciation, certainly, is due in full measure to the photographers—
Rick Lenz, Carl Malotka, Charles Miller, Stan Grayson,
Don Vorderman and Henry Austin Clark, Jr.—who have brought to
life the many cars which appear in this book. As a writer,
I am not quite convinced of the one-picture-is-worth-a-thousand-words theory.
But in this case I would make an exception.

And to David R. Crippen, reference archivist of the Ford Archives,
a special note of thanks for ferreting out in that estimable collection the
portraits and photographs herein of Henry Ford,
as he appeared during the various eras of his car-building career.

Most of all, I am grateful to the memory of Henry Ford.
I wish I had known him. I wish I owned one example of each of the cars
that he built. Neither of those wishes being possible,
the enjoyment of putting together this book will suffice . . . nicely.

Princeton, New Jersey   Beverly Rae Kimes
December, 1977

BY L. SCOTT BAILEY

Today it seems almost bizarre that my earliest years were devoid of any interest in cars. But there were reasons. My boyhood was spent in a sleepy canal town named after Benjamin Franklin in southwestern Ohio, forty miles north of a more exciting port of call where palatial steamboats docked, the Queen City, the gateway to the west, Cincinnati. Cincinnati was "where there was life," as my New York City born and bred mother would lament. It was to Cincinnati that my parents went to buy lamb, oysters, sour cream and wine. Franklin's bill of fare was white beans, white pork and corn bread. It was Cincinnati where good food, theatrical shows and music could be found, as well as "decent clothes." I remember, when I was five, my father saying excitedly once upon his return, "I saw a Pierce-Arrow." For a long time I wasn't sure if it was an Indian or a musical play.

The fact is I detested cars. Hunting crawdads in Sundown Farm's stream, kite flying, a day at the blacksmith shop along the canal, these were the most exciting adventures I could imagine. My first vivid memory of an automobile was of my mother's Ford T going up Second Street hill, making a sharp left-hand turn into our driveway, heading straight for the first under-the-house garage in town, and only missing a collision with the rear wall because of a double row of spare tires. I was in the car at the time. Thereafter, except when my father drove, I would demand being allowed to leave the car after we crossed the canal, so I could make the long walk to the top of the hill "safely."

Life came to Franklin early on Saturday morning, when all the farmers arrived in town, lining the streets with horse and wagons. There were cars amongst them, I vaguely remembered, all looking like dusty blackbirds. I don't ever recall seeing a colorful car in Franklin. It would probably have been out of place in those dull, drab surroundings. But I do remember hearing snatches of talk about cars, most of it ominous. "Clarence broke his arm a-cranking," a farmer's wife told my mother. And, overheard at the slaughter house: "The best way to take the squeak out of those wooden wheels is to drown 'em in the old swimming hole at Twin Creek over a weekend." Such comments, and my mother's continual accident-proneness, convinced me that automobiles were dangerous machines.

Then too, there was the hushed but often-told story of a family friend who lost a fortune by "investing in cars." The investment apparently had been in a nearby Packard agency. Unfortunately, among the Packard owners in Franklin was the proprietor of the steam pressing shop near the canal, the father of a very large family of enterprising sons. His name was Black, as I recall, and years later I was able to reconstruct what had happened. Mr. Black always bought a black and very used Packard, generally a large touring sedan. One summer, to increase his income, he fenced in some pigs on the muddy side of Twin Creek. They had to be fed, of course. So, strapping two large fifty-gallon drums to the trunk rack of the Packard, Mr. Black would collect garbage from the local bars and restaurants to swill the hogs. When the four o'clock whistle blew, Black's Packard would be leading the parade of cars coming from the Logan Long paper mill. It became legend that, when you were shopping for a new car, salesmen invariably would exclaim, "You're not going to buy a swill wagon, are you!" And this led to the demise of the local Packard enthusiasm—and our friend's "investment."

Eventually we moved nearer to the Queen City, to a place of more charm and grace, Middletown, thirty-six miles from Cincinnati. For the first time I began seeing bright and shiny and colorful cars. Cars that weren't mud-covered or lumpy with dents or holed with rust. Cars were interesting after all. I learned that Pierce-Arrow was not an Indian, and Duesenberg wasn't an automobile made in Germany.

At the age of fifteen, I was a budding cub reporter for the *Middletown Journal* and I thought it was extremely necessary that I own a car to fully follow my nose for news. Not far down Central Avenue, across from Boykins' Garage, there sat a used car lot packed with T's, A's and Dodges, with their prices marked in Bon Ami paste paint: $50, $75, $100—a small fortune. My cub reporter job was prestigious, but non-paying. It would lead to a merit badge in journalism for the Boy Scouts and a scholarship for school—but it would not buy a car. So I made my money delivering the *Dayton Daily News*, spending summer afternoons as an assistant to the cook at Jack's Diner across from the P. Lorillard tobacco factory and working as a car hop at the Jug hamburger and root beer drive-in. It was the cook at Jack's who convinced me what car I should buy.

As I peeled potatoes, he lied confidentially about once having been the driver for John Dillinger's mob. He told me that Fords were the fastest getaway cars of all, and that he and Dillinger made many a breathtaking escape from the police or FBI in a Ford. If I was going to buy a car, he said, it must be a Ford. I seem to have forgotten all his other worldly advice, but I always remembered that.

Thus my first car was a Ford, a Model T, a 1927 turtleback roadster bought for $22.50 because its school teacher owner didn't like cranking, rarely drove it, and was retiring and didn't need it anymore anyway. I overhauled it, gave it a shaved head, light pistons, and quick change bands, among other speed accessories provided by Western Auto. I repainted it, pinstriped it in red. True to what I had been told, it would run like the wind.

By the time it was in shape to whip any untuned Model A owned by my contemporaries, I had driven many miles without a license for it or myself. Whenever we had the opportunity, a friend and I would push the T down the street and over to the cindered team tracks of the Big Four railroad and there, on private land and with the kind approval of the B&O freight agent, we would drive and tune and drive and tune all day . . . much to the consternation of the police. With youthful arrogance, I had told the officer on the beat that neither a driver's license nor a vehicle license was required on private land, only public streets and highways. Once, however, the police thought they had us as we were discovered taking the T home, my friend with his shoulder to the rear-mounted spare, me pushing with my left hand and steering with my right. Summoned before the municipal court, I explained, with what confidence I had left, that steering was not driving. The judge dismissed the case.

Not long after, when I was of legal age to do so, I licensed both of us, and

thereafter the T and I spent many miles of pleasurable driving and racing over the country roads and hilly terrain of western Ohio. There were long night rides when my T beat the Model A boys, much to their acute embarrassment. Their revenge was often crude. I became accustomed to potatoes jammed in my T's tailpipe. I always pocketed my distributor, carried a tire pump and checked warily under the tires for large, fat tacks.

The shortest ride I ever took in the turtleback Ford was on the evening I picked up the daughter of the *Middletown Journal*'s advertising manager, with whom I was trying to make points in hopes for a paying job. While headed in the direction of the Paramount Theatre, we were rapidly being overcome by a very powerful and obnoxious odor. Lowering the windows and opening the vent on the cowl was of little help. Finally the prim Mary Margaret said, "Do you smell something?" I had to admit I did. Ultimately, choking and tearing, we were forced to flee the Ford. Next to removing essence of skunk, the removal of limberger cheese spread over a manifold is the most difficult task I have ever attempted.

Eventually the T was traded in on a 1935 V-8. Jack's cook had been right. Its acceleration was fantastically fast. It also drank oil by the barrel. Thirty-two quarts between Middletown and Budd Lake, and the return trip was made in front of a smokescreen of used crankcase oil that was freely and necessarily given with each stop for gas. Its aluminum heads were the most contrary parts I ever tried to separate. But my V-8 stood the test of time and did splendid service in that age of innocence just prior to World War II.

When I was called to service in the Cincinnati Naval Reserve, it sat in the side yard, sheathed with tarps. Eventually it was dismantled to provide replacement parts for neighborhood defense workers' transportation. First went the tires, then the wheels, then the engine—and finally what was left was taken by the local scrap drive for munitions to be hurled at Japan, the country which only a few short years before had bought every available pound of scrap from the United

States to build *its* arsenal. Silly wars. Sillier people who wage them,
only to become closer friends afterwards and allies against other sillier people.

At the end of the war I was a member of the staff at the Submarine School
in New London, Connecticut where, with luck, I bought a Model A sedan for $50
because of the midnight transfer of a shipmate. The Model A was for me,
I thought at first, a step backward in time, if not self esteem. There wasn't much
left of it, but it could be made to run and it was reliable for short trips to
Mystic and Old Lyme. I parked it every night beneath the wall of an abandoned quarry
along the Thames at the entrance to the base. In exchange for small favors,
it was watched over by the Marine guard. On September 4th, 1945, my birthday,
a notice of discharge—written all over with my shipmates' names and best wishes—
was on my desk, instructing me to report to Boston the next day. Naturally jubilant
and in understandable great haste, I took off for that city and the ritual of
discharge. Things began happening very quickly after that.

A month later, in a college dorm in Oxford, Ohio, I suddenly remembered.
My Model A . . . it was still there, at the bottom of that cliff! Or was it? I called
Connecticut to find out. None of my Navy friends remained at the base,
but the Marine guard sent someone over to the area where my A had been parked.
It wasn't there, the space had been taken for military storage. (I never did
trust a Marine.) The Model A had become the first of two Fords during my lifetime
which I would absentmindedly abandon.

During law school, with the help of Peggy, the girl I had just married,
I began publishing law school briefs. They sold like hotcakes and swelled our bank
account to the point where we were able to trade in our 1937 Ford sedan for a dollar
—I wanted a new car badly—plus cash and receive in exchange the first
all-new postwar Ford to arrive in Cincinnati. It was misty green, perky, powerful
and extremely dependable.

But somehow or another, I had never forgotten my first Model T. A car to get
from here to there was fine, but now I began hearing of a brand-new idea
about automobiles: finding old ones, collecting them, restoring them, enjoying them.
What a great notion that was! Clubs had been formed, publications were being
produced for the faithful. I was intrigued.

I can remember on many occasions pointing out to my wife a pile of scrap along
some roadside or in a junkyard, and commenting on its potential restorability.
Peggy was skeptical. In another instance, during supper one evening, she remarked

offhandedly having seen an old car in the local Ford agency in Batavia.
I rushed from the table to check it out. It was a 1927 Model T the Lewis brothers
had restored for their sister to use in making her nursing rounds. It wasn't for sale.
I returned home to the supper my wife had kept warm for me. I could talk
of nothing else but that Model T. Peggy remained skeptical. She didn't understand;
we had a perfectly fine brand-new Ford, what good was a twenty-three-year-old one?
But I think she suspected there might be a change coming to our lives soon.

In 1951 we were at Watkins Glen, New York for the road races, joining the
organizers and supporters of the event, the wives of the drivers and the officials for
a picnic on the back acreage of Sonny Clute's farm overlooking part of the
picturesque circuit. The race was preceded by a parade of old cars. One of them was
an immaculate 1913 brass radiator Model T that chugged to the top of the hill,
steamed and finally boiled over, coming to a stop—fortuitously—right in front of us.
Its owner, Dick Raitt, went off for water, and my wife leaned over to me and said,
"Now if you really want an old car, why don't you get something like that?"
That was all the encouragement I needed. By the time Dick had reached the water pump,
I had made up my mind; by the time he returned to the Model T, I was ready to
negotiate my first purchase of an antique automobile. It was the beginning of a
collection, the first of some thirty old cars I would buy, many of them Fords.

The second was a Ford too and a particularly poignant story was attached to it.
It was a center-door T belonging to a kindly old man in Elmira, New York
where we had moved in 1950. He was a neat little fellow, stooped and shrunken with age,
his clothes hanging loosely around him. But he had such dignity. He took
me out to his garage, which was as tidy as he was, and the Model T which like its
owner was a little withered by its years but which obviously had been treated
with tender care since the day in 1919 when it was originally purchased. The old man
loved that car, I recognized that simply from the way he looked at it.
Why do you want to sell it? I asked him. I have to, he replied wistfully, my children
insist, they say I'm too old to drive it, they've taken my driver's license
away from me, they've hidden the car's license plate too. I think $100 was the
purchase price, absurdly low now, a reasonable price then. But I felt a little guilty
parting this man from his car. Maybe I wouldn't have to . . . completely.
Look, I said, I don't really have a ready place to keep the car, could I leave it
here in your garage? His eyes beamed, his back straightened. He became young again.
Oh yes, he replied, I'll keep the battery up and the dust off, don't you worry.

Some time later Peggy and I had moved again, to Long Island—and in the rush
of events, the press of business, the collection of belongings scattered far and wide,
I forgot all about the T. Until in conversation one evening at a party
with some enthusiast friends, the subject of center-door T's came up. Good grief . . .

suddenly I remembered. I phoned Elmira. The old man had died. He's been gone a long time now, I was informed, the house has been sold and the garage is empty. I don't know whatever happened to that Model T, but I'm sure that kindly little man looked after it until the end.

I guess my favorite among all the Fords we owned was the Model F Peg and I saw in a barn in Vermont. With the help of Hank Edmonds and Owen Bombard of the Ford Archives, Elmer Bemis of Brattleboro restored it to precisely the way it had looked when it left the Ford factory in 1905. It was exquisite, it won the coveted Thompson Products award, an AACA National First Prize and numerous other trophies. But driving it was the most fun; it would do a genuine 50 mph, and for hours on end. Not bad for a two-cylinder car. Peggy captioned the back of one of our pictures of it, "October 1957 at Luray, Virginia, after traveling 900 miles in two days." Before it finally came to a well-deserved rest in D.E. Fagan's private Ford museum, we had driven well over 5000 miles in that car, including a Glidden Tour and a trek from Rochester, New York, via Canada, to Detroit for the annual Henry Ford Museum meet.

On the Glidden, we had enjoyed lunch in Hershey, Pennsylvania with publisher Floyd Clymer and Austin Clark, Bill Pollock and other veterans of what was now a burgeoning old car movement. We all agreed that there was a need for a book about the hobby and Peg and I were asked if we would like to write one. Floyd said to send him something to look at, that he'd be interested in publishing it. So on the trip out for the Ford meet, as we coursed through Canada in the Model F, sans windshield, doors or overhead covering, Peg took down in shorthand a general outline, chapter heads and topical sentences. On the return trip to New York, we filled in the empty spaces and at home typed it all up. With the help of friends from the Antique Automobile Club, the Horseless Carriage Club, the Veteran Motor Car Club as well as the Veteran Car Club of Great Britain, we gathered together photographs and other material and compiled a listing of about two thousand automobiles that had been manufactured in the United States since the 1890's.

We packaged the results and sent them to Floyd, noting that it was, as he asked, something to look at, unedited and roughly written but a general idea of what the book might be. Floyd took it to a printer to get an estimate of what the book would cost to produce in a specific number of pages—and then he took off for Europe. Unfortunately, the printer misunderstood the instructions because Floyd returned from the Continent to find the book printed, just as it was. Well, almost as it was. The page count for the book was reached midway through the list we had compiled of marques manufactured in the United States—so the roster ended rather abruptly in the middle of the S's.

Buy An Antique Car was published in 1958. Today, twenty years later, whenever I leaf through it, I can only smile at the naivete we all had in those days. After I entered the field myself and published the first book in AUTOMOBILE *Quarterly*'s Library Series, *The American Car Since 1775*, I saw to it that the roster of American cars therein—five thousand of them this time—went all the way to Z and the Zip cyclecar.

But another thing hasn't changed. *Buy An Antique Car* had as its subtitle: "A Handbook for Those Interested in the World's Most Fascinating Hobby." The years have not altered that for me. What was altered was the course of my life. Doubtless whatever had happened, I would be a publisher today. Publishing had fascinated me since early boyhood when I brought out my first publication, a neighborhood newsletter. Perhaps I'd be publishing about art or history now . . . save for the Model T.

It was the Model T which had introduced me to the fascination of cars, and again it would be the Model T about which I first wrote extensively. And nothing was the same after that. In 1951 Jerry Duryea, son of Charles E. and nephew of J. Frank, asked me—as a member of the Antique Automobile Club of America— to contribute a column, "Model T Topics," to the club's publication. This I did, and thereafter I became a member of the organization's executive board and eventually volunteer editor of *Antique Automobile*. I saw it grow during the next five years from a subscription roll of three thousand to some fourteen thousand. With the addition of two more issues per year and more advertising pages per issue, a full-time editor could be employed as well as a professional business manager. The hobby was growing incredibly.

It was about this time—more than seventeen years ago now—that Peggy and I sat down one evening and thought out the AUTOMOBILE *Quarterly* idea. We would launch a hardbound magazine dedicated to the history of the automobile. It was a decision neither of us has ever regretted. It has enriched our lives.

And it all started with a Ford. Oh, the memories the pages that follow bring back to me. Here is a brass T just like the one we bought at Watkins Glen, a V-8 like the one in which I tried to out-Dillinger Dillinger, a Model A like the one left in that quarry, a center-door T like our Elmira car, and a Model F to recall those thousands of marvelous touring miles and all the fun we had.

It is with pride certainly, but more than that, it is a sentimental pleasure to publish this book.

There are no doubt people abroad in this land who continue to believe that Henry Ford invented the automobile, and still others who regard the Model T as Henry's first car. Such is the overwhelming magnitude of both the man and his most famous car. Through the years, in truth, there have sporadically appeared promptings to sustain the legends. The Ford Motor Company itself assisted in this in a 1917 catalogue, commenting about the Model T, straight-faced and straight-from-Genesis, that "In the beginning was the Ford car, and the Ford car was right." And who would likely forget — once having seen it — the photograph in that *Life* magazine of 1947, showing Henry Ford lying in repose, below which a headline spread starkly across the page: "The Father of the Automobile Dies." The photograph is a haunting one, two Ford workmen, still in factory clothes, gazing almost awestruck at the man who gave the world the Model T, the all-consuming reality of mass production, the startling concept of five dollars for a day's work.

But our story does not begin with that Henry Ford. Not Henry Ford the folk hero. Nor Henry the Vilified — as he was both in life and death: Like all men he was oft fallible, and his mistakes, like his triumphs, were big ones. Nor are his politics, his prejudices, his peculiarities, his peace ship — all fascinating avenues repeatedly traveled by historians in search of the real Henry Ford — of concern right now. Instead we shall first examine the Henry Ford who was not larger than life, whose renown extended not much further than that of many other automotive pioneers. Even Henry Ford had to start somewhere.

The beginnings were unremarkable enough. Born July 30th, 1863, in rural Michigan, Ford grew up as a farm boy who didn't like farming. His father William Ford would later quote neighbors referring to him as a lad "with wheels in his head" — and in this he was really no different from many another boy during those thriving years of the Industrial Age. School was a bore, he learned neither to spell nor to express himself well in writing; penmanship and facility in reading escaped him. Still the *McGuffey's Readers* that were his schoolbooks had a lasting influence, and later years would find him often turning an epigrammatic hand to such sagacities as "Health is catching." (Ben Franklin had nothing on Henry Ford.)

But even McGuffey was not long to distract young Henry from such ambitious ventures as the building of a water wheel, and a stab at the construction of a steam turbine. Both those experiments ended spectacularly, the former causing a considerable flood in a neighbor's potato patch and the latter exploding and setting fire to the school fence. Henry's father, fortunately, possessed sainted patience, wincing barely perceptibly at his son's mechanical antics — and when young Henry, aged sixteen, left his native Springwells-Dearborn to travel the few miles to Detroit in 1879, William Ford acquiesced, in the belief perhaps that young Henry's preoccupation with matters mechanical was, like young love, but a passionate, sometimes painful and fleeting part of growing up.

In a way then, Henry Ford was never to leave his adolescence. Clearly already he was demonstrating those qualities of pugnacious persistence and plain bullheadedness about which the world would later create legends. His first job lasted six days. His short sojourn with the streetcar-building Michigan Car Com-

FROM CLARA'S KITCHEN SINK TO HIGHLAND PARK

pany at Grand Truck Junction provided but one lesson; as Henry later said, "I learned then not to tell all you know." What apparently happened was that the young mechanic had the audacity to effect certain repairs in something like ten-percent of the time required by practiced hands — and such fearsome efficiency was enough to cause him either to be fired, or to resign in lieu thereof. Even as a teenager Henry Ford was perhaps his own best boss. Nonetheless he was almost immediately back on employment rolls, this time at the James Flowers & Brothers Machine Shop on Woodbridge and Bush streets, his father more than likely having opened the door. (The Ford and Flowers families were friends.) There, for sixty hours and $2.50 a week, Henry apprenticed — augmenting his income by two dollars weekly with night work repairing clocks and watches at the McGill Jewelry Store on Baker Street, and using whatever time was left to voraciously consume just about everything that was being written about the new gasoline engine developments of a certain Nikolaus August Otto in Germany. At the conclusion of nine months — in late summer of 1880 — Henry Ford left Flowers, took a fifty-cent-per-week cut in pay and went to work for Detroit's largest shipbuilding firm, the Detroit Drydock Company. The move was made deliberately to gain experience, and young Henry got plenty of it, working constantly in the engine department with a variety of powerplants. He remained there two years.

Eighteen eighty-two found Henry back on the farm, at least insofar as it would serve as a postal address and sometimes residence. His father had expected that his son, aged nineteen, would now be, literally, shopworn, weary of the mechanical life after toiling at it for several years in Detroit machine shops. No such luck. For a time Henry worked for the Westinghouse Engine Company of Schenectady, New York, servicing that firm's traction engines used by southern Michigan farmers; he attended awhile the Goldsmith, Bryant & Stratton Business University in Detroit; he repaired an Otto engine at the Eagle Iron Works in that city — and he met and courted a lovely young girl by the name of Clara Jane Bryant, the daughter of a Greenfield township farmer.

For a while it appears Henry's obsession with mechanics took a back seat to his romantic interest, and when his father offered him a tract of heavily-timbered land near the Ford farm — the old Moir place — in exchange for giving up being a machinist, young Henry "agreed in a provisional way, for cutting timber gave me a chance to get married." He built a sawmill, cleared the land, sold the timber. He also married Clara, on April 11th, 1888.

Within a year the Fords were comfortably ensconced in a new home on the Moir place, Henry farming a bit of the cleared land and actively plying his sawmill trade. But Henry had also built and equipped what he called "a first class workshop." He had by now progressed considerably from those boyhood days when he fashioned such tools as a pair of tweezers from a corset stay, a screw driver by filing the point of a shingle nail — and when, upon finding a clock requiring repair, he promptly took it apart. Jokingly a neighbor had said at the time that every clock in the Ford home shuddered when it saw him coming. One might suspect that Clara was now having similar quavers, as she saw her husband spending less and less time in agrarian pursuits and more and more in his fine new shop — or in Detroit whenever a repair job called him there.

Late in the summer of 1891 Henry returned from a repair job of an Otto engine at a Detroit soda bottling plant, sat Clara down, told her he was convinced such an engine could be adapted to a road-going vehicle, but before he could do it he needed some experience with electricity, and that an engineering job was awaiting

him at the Edison Illuminating Company in Detroit. Faced with what was apparently a *fait accompli*, one which would disrupt their orderly lives, and all because of a notion for a vehicle that to her was certainly mind-boggling, Clara acceded, unflinching. Clara Bryant Ford was the archetype of the traditional good wife: She had unwavering faith in her husband and was convinced that if such an unlikely vehicle could be built, Henry could build it. And she never doubted the importance of trying.

And so on September 25th, 1891, the Fords moved to Detroit — and Henry joined that coterie of American inventors actively pursuing the idea of harnessing the power of the internal combustion engine to a road vehicle. Eighteen ninety-three was to conclude momentously for the Fords; on November 6th their first and only child, Edsel, was born; on December 1st, Henry was promoted to chief engineer of the Edison company, and on Christmas Eve Henry tested his first gasoline engine. Actually Henry *and* Clara conducted that first test. The engine was a makeshift, and somewhat incomplete, affair — a reamed out one-inch gas pipe serving as the cylinder, into which fitted a homemade piston carrying a rod to the crankshaft with a five-inch stroke. An old lathe supplied the flywheel, and the engine was equipped with a gear to activate a cam, opening the exhaust valve and timing the spark. House current was to supply the electricity — and the engine lacked a carburetor. Gasoline had to be dribbled into the intake valve by hand; that was Clara's job. The flywheel had to be spun for starting; that was Henry's. Somehow the engine sputtered to life, which was all its inventor wanted to find out; after a minute or two it was allowed to die — and Henry took it away from the kitchen sink where the test had taken place and allowed Clara to return to her preparations for Christmas dinner. Clara Ford, it bears repeating, was an extraordinary woman.

About this time Henry Ford had made the acquaintance of Charles Brady King, erstwhile engineer of the Michigan Car Company, inventor of a pneumatic hammer and lately organizer of the Charles B. King Company. It was King who was to relay to Henry a first-hand account of the goings-on at the *Chicago Times-Herald* race of 1895 — which news no doubt even more convinced Henry of the wisdom of his horseless carriage idea. But King was to beat him to it. When King first publicly demonstrated his car in Detroit on March 6th, 1896, Henry Ford was cycling behind; King's was, after all, the first gasoline car he had ever seen.

But Henry was already well on his way to coming up with his own car, with advice from King and assistance from a couple of his Edison company associates. The January 3rd, 1896 issue of the *American Machinist* had featured an illustrated article on the Kane-Pennington engine, which Henry used as a guide, although he was to deviate considerably from it. The new Ford engine was a horizontal in-line four-cycle two-cylinder affair measuring 2½ by 6 inches and displacing 59 cubic inches; with a compression ratio of about 3:1, it produced an output estimated at around four horsepower. Ignition was low-tension coil make-and-break and a manually-operated needle valve served for carburetion. Initially air cooled, the engine overheated during its first tests and brazed water jackets were then fitted. Leather belts and pulleys transmitted the power from the engine to a transverse jackshaft.

Next came the chassis and body, both extremely light in weight — in toto, the entire machine, sans fuel, would weigh but 500 pounds. The frame was fashioned of four two-by-two rails (later replaced with angle iron); the front axle was a drop type, the rear one piece with a differential arrangement not unlike that of some contemporary steam traction engines. The exposed differential gears were outboard of the frame, adjacent to the right rear wheel, with the drive sprocket receiving power via chain. A bicycle seat and bicycle wheels were fitted, both eventually to be discarded.

All this, of course, occupied much of Henry's time through the spring of 1896 — his moments of frustration buoyed by his dear Clara's steadfast belief that he would succeed. Said Henry later: "It was a very great thing to have my wife even more confident than I was." Clara was also very good at keeping a secret; when friends visited she'd make frequent trips out to the machine shop shed in back to check her husband's progress, only to return and tantalize her guests with "Henry is making something, and maybe some day I'll tell you."

By early June the secret was out, so was the car — and so was most of the side of the shed in which it was built. Henry had tended to disregard that what was built within had eventually to be taken out—a strongly wielded axe solved that. It was the Fords' landlord who later, after his initial anger subsided, suggested that instead of restoring said shed to its original condition, that the opening be left as was and a wider door be installed. Henry later insisted the result was America's first garage door.

The historic import of that episode, however, pales in light of the little Ford's first run — an exultant trip made before dawn on June 4th, with Henry at the tiller, associate Jim Bishop cycling behind, the pair making a side excursion to the Edison plant to pick up a spring to replace one broken in the ignition en route, driving back to the Ford Bagley Street home, catching a little sleep, being served breakfast by Clara and then casually reporting for work at the Edison company as usual.

Continued improvements to the quadricycle followed; what had originally been wood in the vehicle (which comprised just about everything except the engine, axle, wheels and steering gear) was largely replaced by metal, adding about 175 pounds to the car's overall weight. Now strengthened and with the addition of a buggy seat to replace the bicycle variety used on the first test trip, Henry could have company as he drove. His most frequent passenger was Clara who would sit serenely with Edsel on her lap as Henry tootled off to the country (either to the Ford or Bryant farm), neighbors remarking all the while on her surprising equanimity. Henry's father William, however, was less enthusiastic; he had taken his son's decision for the mechanical rather than the rural life without much complaint, but still he viewed the Ford quadricycle as a plaything, and was more than a little embarrassed. Young Henry was now thirty-three years old, after all, and ought to be settling down.

In August of 1896 Henry Ford was sent to New York as a delegate to the seventeenth annual convention of the Association of Edison Illuminating Companies, during which time he met and talked with Thomas Alva Edison, drew his automotive ideas on the back of a menu for that great gentleman and elicited from him a thumping, "Young man, that's the thing! You have it. Keep at it!" With the most ringing endorsement of his efforts yet — save, of course, for Clara's — Henry returned home more determined than ever and told his wife, "You won't be seeing much of me for the next year."

Although he hadn't originally intended to sell the quadricycle, he did — to one Charles Ainsley — and the $200 it brought was helpful in getting Henry started on his second vehicle. He also received aid from an old friend, William C. Maybury, the mayor of Detroit who earlier, after the quadricycle had stirred some protest from city residents, officially, but probably only verbally, issued Henry permission to use the vehicle on city streets. Henry would later comment,

". . . thus for a time I enjoyed the distinction of being the only licensed chauffeur in America." (Fancying himself "the first" or "the only" was to become a Ford penchant.)

Henry Ford was, by this time, thinking big; his second vehicle was to be but a stepping stone: "It was not at all my idea to make cars in any such petty fashion," he later said. Still that prototype did have to be built, and Maybury came through with additional financing, both of his own and from several other investors — Ellery I. Garfield, E.A. Leonard, Benjamin R. Hoyt — whom he contacted on Ford's behalf.

Just when Henry completed this second vehicle is a puzzlement, perhaps late 1897, perhaps early 1898. The first press indication of the venture was a short three-sentence mention in an issue of *Horseless Age* in November of 1898. It was reported therein that Henry was "financially supported by several prominent men of the city" — true — and that he had "built a number of gasoline vehicles which are said to have been successfully operated" — certainly not true, if one considers "a number" constituting more than two. Interesting, though, was the last sentence: "From Mr. Ford himself no information can be gleaned regarding his vehicles or his plans for their manufacture." Apparently Henry did not feel ready to publicize his efforts, most likely because he was not yet satisfied with the results. His first test run with the quadricycle, significantly, had gone unreported as well.

Sometime early in 1899, however, all this changed. Henry had met William H. Murphy the Wealthy, and Murphy had promised assistance if Henry could drive him from his Detroit home to Farmington and then back by way of Pontiac. Henry could, and did — several months later. Murphy was sufficiently impressed with the ride to offer to form a company to manufacture a Ford car. Maybury and his associates were amenable, and so on July 24th the Detroit Automobile Company was organized, comprising the aforementioned gentlemen as well as such other financial luminaries as Clarence A. Black, Albert E. F. White, Mark Hopkins, William C. McMillan, Frank R. Alderman, Lem Bowen and F. W. Eddy. To give an idea of the fiscal integrity of the new company, one need only mention that the McMillans and the Murphys pretty much owned downtown Detroit. Now all Henry had to do was come through with a design suitable for production. He resigned his position with the Edison company to take superintendency of the new Detroit firm, with facilities at 1343-1355 Cass Avenue. He would be a small stockholder in the company, although he did not himself invest any money.

The Ford car was given a splashy spread in the *Detroit Journal* of July 29th, 1899—by that time it was, of course, more than a year old, and the news value of the piece was tempered. Its content, too, would indicate that the magnetic charm which detractors would years hence insist Henry Ford did not have had left an impression on the *Journal* reporter. Barefacedly he extolled the car's "new" features — which in reality were not — and Ford's noble endeavors to avoid the mistakes of his predecessors. ("The French inventors had gone to the extreme of heaviness in construction and had apparently only one idea and that to get a wagon that would run without horses.") Ford's car weighed 875 pounds, but Henry promised to bring that down to 800 in the marketable version.

Still, Henry's next vehicle — a delivery wagon — was heavier still: 1200 pounds. And despite the theatrical allure of the headline in *The Detroit News-Tribune* of February 4th, 1900 — "SWIFTER THAN A RACEHORSE IT FLEW OVER THE ICY STREETS" — the vehicle was rather dreadful, as breakable as a Christmas toy and just as difficult to repair.

The first Ford, the 1896 Quadricycle / Henry Ford Museum

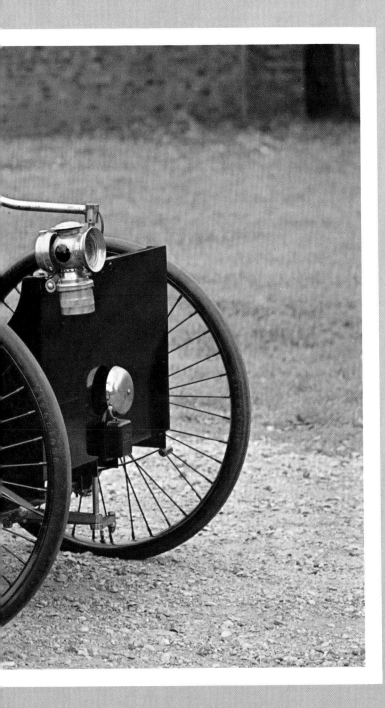

Production simply wasn't forthcoming. Part of the problem was delay in or inferior quality of parts arriving at the shop, part of it too the inexperience of the workmen, part of it Henry Ford who really couldn't make up his mind. With an appealing innocence, Frank Alderman remarked to a reporter in February, "You would be surprised at the amount of detail about an automobile." Apparently everyone at the Detroit Automobile Company was.

In late 1899 Henry had commented to an acquaintance that he had "one and a half [cars] started," by early 1900 perhaps as many as seven were in some stage of planning; maybe a dozen more—at most—followed. But it was, as Henry himself had said, in "petty fashion." After spending $86,000 the Detroit Automobile Company had little to show for it — and soon after celebrating the company's first birthday, the organizers decided not to stick it out for the second. That is, *some* of the organizers.

The official dissolution of the Detroit company was announced in January of 1901. Murphy, however, together with Messrs. Black, Bowen, Hopkins and White, had not yet lost faith. They purchased the company assets and installed Henry back at Cass Avenue, albeit in more modest quarters, and told him to keep working. They assumed he would come up with something. He did — to their dismay. It was a racing car.

To Henry Ford, the decision to go racing was the only logical one he felt could be made. One can't say he was intent on improving the breed, because a truly viable Ford production car hadn't yet been bred, but one might assume he felt the pursuit of speed would solve that. (It was a theory, in any case, which would subsequently enjoy considerable vogue.) Racing, moreover, would call attention to the Ford name and car — Henry was finally becoming publicity conscious — and that could only prove beneficial. And one might presume, too, that Henry simply liked the idea.

And so a car was built—a 1600-pound machine (comparatively light for racers of that day) powered by a two-cylinder opposed engine with a bore and stroke of seven inches displacing some 540 cubic inches, developing some 26 horsepower and capable of a raucous 900 revolutions per minute. Oliver Barthel, who formerly had been associated with Charles Brady King and who had been working with Ford for some time, worked closely with Henry on its design. Henry was revved up. This Ford racing interlude would also bring to the company such pioneers in the automotive art as Edward S. "Spider" Huff, Ed Ver Linden and subsequently, and very significantly, Childe Harold Wills, a young man who had learned his machinist trade in several Detroit machine shops during daylight hours, and who had spent his evenings studying chemistry, engineering and metallurgy. Obviously ambitious, Wills saw Henry Ford as a man who was going places and he wanted to go along.

Two things Henry wanted initially — to beat Henri Fournier who was making loud noises in the East with his Paris-Berlin-winning Mors (which would culminate in November with a flying mile record of 69.5 mph) and to beat Alexander Winton for the sheer joy of it. Alexander Winton, of course, was America's premier racer and the record holder of most distances up to twenty-five miles. Henry took on Winton first — on October 10th, 1901, at the Grosse Pointe race track. Various prizes were slated for the event, including for the twenty-five-mile sweepstakes, $1000 in cash (somehow it would never be awarded) and an exquisite cut glass punch bowl which had been selected because "it would look well in the bay window of the Winton dining room." No doubt then who was supposed to win that race. Two cars only competed: Winton's and Ford's. Henry made a

Henry's second car, 1898 / Henry Ford Museum

Henry's fourth car, 1901 / Henry Ford Museum

Henry's first racing car, 1901 / Henry Ford Museum

two-lap warm-up run with the famous cyclist Tom Cooper, Cooper purportedly giving the novice racing driver advice on the track and how to course it most efficiently. Then Spider Huff took his mechanic's seat beside Henry, and the contest was on. A little less than thirteen-and-a-half minutes later Henry had won his first race. Clara wrote her brother: "I wish you could have seen him. Also have heard the cheering when he passed Winton. The people went wild. One man threw his hat up and when it came down he stamped on it, he was so excited. Another man had to hit his wife on the head to keep her from going off the handle. She stood up in her seat [and] screamed 'I'd bet fifty dollars on Ford if I had it.' They were friends of ours." Now the only problem was the punch bowl; as Clara lamented, "Well of all things to win. . . . Where will we ever put it?"

Scarcely had the dust settled from the race than Henry's suddenly enthusiastic backers decided that a new company definitely was in order. This time it would be called the Henry Ford Company, the articles of incorporation being filed on November 30th. As Clara wrote: "That [Grosse Pointe] race had advertised him far and wide. And the next thing will be to make some money out of it. I am afraid that will be a hard struggle. You know rich men want it all." What the rich men wanted, naturally, was to manufacture automobiles, but their company engineer had something else in mind. As Henry wrote his brother on January 6th, 1902: "If I can bring Mr. Fournier in line [Ford had met the French ace in New York and hoped to team with him] there is a barrel of money in this business it was his proposition and I don't see why he won't fall in line if he don't I will chalenge him untill I am black in the face. . . . My Company will kick about me following racing but they will get the advertising and I expect to make $ where I can't make cs at manufacturing." Within three months Henry was out of the Henry Ford Company.

The directors had been desperate to get into production, Henry wasn't ready; they had decreed that a racer could not be built on company time, Henry was furious; earlier they had brought in one Henry Martyn Leland as a consultant, Henry grew aghast. Leland, subsequently the designer of the first Cadillac and Lincoln motorcars, was a perfectionist, that master of precision who would bring the principle of interchangeability of parts to the automobile industry. He was working at his Leland and Faulconer Company at the time, but as a Ford associate would recall, "he used to come over and see Mr. Ford and his car. He would talk about it and criticize it to Mr. Murphy. I think that made Mr. Ford mad." Indubitably. The Leland affair was really the capstone; Henry Ford's authority was being challenged. He left summarily, taking with him only the drawings for the new racer, a $900 settlement, Murphy's promise to drop the name "Henry Ford" and a resolve "never again to put myself under orders."

"Henry is making arrangement for quitting everything and taking hold of racing," Clara wrote her brother on March 3rd, 1902. Indeed Henry was. By early May, Ford had fresh money—Tom Cooper's. Cooper had been vastly impressed by the Ford effort at Grosse Pointe, and was willing to underwrite the building of not one but two racers, one apiece ostensibly. "Tom Cooper . . . has got the racing fever bad," commented Clara.

The two men set up shop at 81 Park Place, and out of it bellowed two legendary cars: 999 and the Arrow. The cars were identical, the former—named for the popular New York Central express train—being completed first. Aesthetics played no part in the design of 999; it was a brute. Four cylinders of 7¼ by 7 inches for a displacement of 1155.3 cubic inches. Horsepower quoted at 100 by the *Detroit Journal*, although Henry modestly admitted to seventy or eighty. A wheelbase of

The 999 racer, 1902 / Henry Ford Museum

109 inches, track measuring fifty-six. The idea was to most effectively utilize power, this accomplished by dispensing with a differential, the engine driving the rear axle directly by means of bevel gears. Not provided either were transmission change gears, a flywheel clutch disconnecting the motor from the wheels. And it was all there for everyone to see—every part of it, naked to the world. As *The Automobile and Motor Review* noted engagingly in late September 1902: "Built for speed and speed alone, the two new racing machines . . . are first-class examples of how an automobile may be simplified by the 'leaving off' process. This most recent addition to the ranks of racing monsters has power and means to apply it; it has few conveniences, no luxuries and not the slightest indication of a frill or decoration. Not even has an attempt been made to hide the machinery, for a motor-bonnet is not necessary to speed, and no other considerations matter."

A tiller would steer the vehicle, Henry concluded, reasoning this a safety factor: "You see, when the machine is making high speed, and the operator cannot tell because of dust . . . whether he is going perfectly straight, he can look at this steering handle. If it is set straight across the machine he is all right. . ." Where this left the operator in a curve apparently wasn't considered. Finally, a single seat was fitted: "One life to a car was enough," said Henry ominously.

Henry tried out the car, as did Cooper. Henry's conclusion: "Going over Niagara Falls would have been but a pasttime" comparatively. Neither Cooper nor Ford were enthralled with the idea of racing the car themselves. Tom Cooper told reporters he anticipated "notable slaughter of the short-distance marks," but apparently neither of the men behind 999 relished risking the same happening to them. They looked around for someone who would. He was quickly found: a cyclist whom the press knew only as B. Oldfield of Toledo. Barney Oldfield had never driven an automobile, but he announced his willingness to try anything once. He tried 999 for a week—just before the Manufacturers' Challenge Cup at Grosse Pointe to be held October 25th, 1902. Then he declared himself ready: ". . . this chariot may kill me, but they will say afterwards that I was going like hell when she took me over the bank."

It was a banner day. Barney trampled all before him at Grosse Pointe, Winton included. Although the feisty Scotsman declared afterwards that the ignition of his racing machine had been tampered with before the race and was the cause of his loss, few really believed that. Barney Oldfield and 999 had simply been spectacular. His time for the five-lap five-miler had been 5:28, a record which he subsequently lowered to 5:20, then 5:15 2/5. He did a mile in 1:01 1/5 in December of 1902, and six months later—on June 19th, 1903—he became the first driver to circle a one-mile track in less than a minute: 59.6 seconds to be exact. A star had been born.

Soon after that October 25th event Cooper and Henry Ford parted company, which dismayed Clara not at all. ("He thinks too much of low down women to suit me.") The two cars remained with Cooper, Henry having sold his to his former partner and Cooper subsequently forming a partnership with Oldfield. Barney spent a season barnstorming the country, driving sometimes 999, on other occasions the Arrow (with Cooper or another driver piloting the other car) in staged exhibitions that would tend to make one believe his real name might have been P. T. Barney. When Winton came up with a faster car, Barney summarily switched allegiance.

Interestingly, Henry Ford had said, following 999's highly successful competition debut, that should Winton ever build such a car, he would "go him one better if I have to design a cylinder as big as a hogshead." But by now his thoughts had

The Model A, 1903 / Henry Ford Museum

The Model B, 1905 / Henry Ford Museum

The Model C, 1904 / Owner: Richard E. Williams

been turned once again to a production car. He had met Alexander Young Malcomson.

Malcomson was a prosperous coal merchant whose product ("Hotter than Sunshine") had long kept Henry and Clara comfortable through the bitter Detroit winters. The two men had met during Henry's Edison company days, when the young engineer was charged with the task of buying the electrical firm's coal supply—and an acquaintance grew into friendship. Malcomson had subsequently become interested in motoring, had purchased a Winton car which he drove spiritedly and, not surprising, had become enthused with the ideas of the man who had built a car that was faster. In August of 1902 Malcomson and Henry Ford signed their first agreement, whereby the merchant was to supply funds for, among other provisions, the development of a marketable automobile. A corporation was to replace the partnership once production seemed imminent; for the moment, however, business commitments dictated that Malcomson's interest in the venture be kept as quiet as possible: All bills would be paid by and under the name of Malcomson's associate, one James Couzens. As for Henry and Clara, they would be living on their savings. Clara still had plenty of faith.

By now C. H. Wills was Henry's most trusted and valuable assistant (it was Wills who would later design the famous Ford trademark), and while Henry and Spider Huff had been busy much of the summer with the racers, the proposed production car was being developed too. By October — during which month 999 had made its eye-popping debut — the little shop at 81 Park Place was, as Malcomson commented, "taking on quite a business aspect." A small but competent work force had been hired — and the pilot production car was nearing completion. A total of some $7000 had been expended.

In November, Malcomson and Ford took the next step: the formation of the Ford & Malcomson Company, Ltd. Of its 15,000 shares, the partners would take 6900 as payment for everything accomplished up to that time, and an additional 350 shares for a $3500 cash investment. Remaining were 7750 shares to be sold — but to whom? One month later, in December, Malcomson arranged for a wagon shop along the belt line railroad at Mack Avenue to be rebuilt into an assembly plant for the forthcoming arrival of running gear, bodies, tires and wheels — but from whom?

The mortality rate of automobile companies, as well as the morality of many speculators shilling stock in those days, was sufficient to make automotive investment a dicey proposition at best. That was generally — specifically, with regard to Henry Ford, his record of accomplishment thus far in the automotive business was certainly less than inspiring. Potential investors stayed away in droves — and those respectfully approached by James Couzens were often brusquely negative. After one particularly wracking interview, Couzens reportedly left the building, sat down on the curb and cried. The last laugh, however, would be his.

Laughing, too, would be the Dodge brothers, who took on a contract with Henry rather than accepting offers made by the Olds and Great Northern companies, both of which at the time had to be considered sounder financial risks. But John F. and Horace E. — a roistering duo who drank and fought well and often — were quite canny businessmen, impressed both by Henry Ford's design, his ideas and his potential. Despite any subsequent unpleasantness, the Dodge brothers would grow rich with Ford. As for Henry, he had the advantage of contracting with one of the biggest shops in the Midwest—how propitious for a beginner in the industry. On February 28th, 1903, the Dodges and the Malcomson & Ford Company entered into an agreement whereby the brothers would

supply chassis and running gear (at $250 each) for 650 automobiles. Subsequent contracts went to the C. R. Wilson Carriage Company (for "wooden bodies with cushions," $68 each); the Hartford Rubber Company (for tires at $40 for four); and the Prudden Company of Lansing (for wheels at $26 a set). The completed Ford car was to sell for $750 in runabout form, $850 for tonneau, with a profit margin estimated at $200 and $150 respectively.

Contracts were going out, unfortunately, faster than investments were coming in, though the ranks of Ford believers now had extended to various members of Malcomson's family, business and social circles. Still, when the $5000 due to the Dodges on March 15th was found lacking and the brothers pressed for payment of it, as they would no doubt the next $5000 due on April 15th, clearly something had to be done. To the rescue came John S. Gray — erstwhile candy tycoon, banker and uncle to Malcomson — who exchanged the needed $10,000, plus an additional $500, for 105 shares of stock and the Ford company presidency. Gray's confidence in the enterprise was never substantial, however. Until his death in 1906 he remained convinced that "this business cannot last"—and the only reason he didn't sell his stock was his conscientious unwillingness to unload it on his friends. By 1915 his estate had received $10,000,000 in dividends alone.

So on June 16th the Ford Motor Company was organized. It absorbed Ford & Malcomson, and left by the wayside the Fordmobile Company, Ltd., the latter having been advertised in trade papers by Malcomson, though there is no evidence it ever proceeded beyond the printed page. The Ford investors numbered twelve, Malcomson and Ford sharing 510 of the 1000 shares of stock, and the remainder divided among Gray, the Dodges, Albert Strelow, Vernon C. Fry, C. H. Bennett, Horace H. Rackham, John W. Anderson, Charles J. Woodall and James Couzens, all either familial or familiar to Malcomson.

Of the $100,000 in stock issued, just $28,000 was paid up in cash — and not all at once. The Ford bank balance in mid-June was some $14,500, whittled down by early July to $223.65. A car as yet had not been sold, and creditors, while not beating down the door, could clearly be heard outside. On July 11th, however, one recalcitrant stockholder (Strelow) came through with a check to cover his stock subscription — and on the 15th one Dr. E. Pfennig of Chicago entered into immortality as the first Ford customer, his check for $850 being joyously deposited in the Ford bank account. It was the first of many to come to the company that month.

Trouble came that month, too, the very day, so legend has it, that Henry Ford and James Couzens— "coats off, collars unbuttoned, sleeves rolled up"—were assisting in the loading of the initial batch of Ford Model A's into freight cars bound for points south and west. Brought to them that day was a Detroit newspaper with an advertisement by the Association of Licensed Automobile Manufacturers, calling the public's attention to its twenty-six licensed firms, its Selden patent and the fact that anyone contemplating the building or selling of a gasoline automobile without a license had better think otherwise—or face prosecution for patent infringement. Never one to take a threat lightly, Henry Ford answered that advertisement two days later—on July 28th—with one of his own in the Detroit *Free Press*. Believing perhaps that one bit of the preposterous deserved another, the ad, over the signature of the Ford Motor Company, noted in part: "We are the pioneers of the GASOLINE AUTOMOBILE. Our Mr. Ford made the first Gasoline Automobile in Detroit and the third in the United States. His machine made in 1893 is still in use." The approximation to truth here was rather tenuous, but then so was the Selden patent. The ad promised to "dealers, importers, agents and users of gasoline automobiles" protection against prosecution for "alleged infringement of patents," and quoted two prominent attorneys as declaring the Selden patent virtually worthless.*

Significantly, Henry Ford had earlier looked—at least twice—into the matter of obtaining a license. The first time he was rebuffed by A.L.A.M. president Frederick L. Smith as a mere assembler, not a manufacturer of automobiles. The second meeting between the two—held probably in June of 1903—was similarly insulting to Ford, Smith implying a fly-by-night character to the Ford company, along with a host of other patronizing poses and postures. Finally James Couzens suggested in no uncertain terms just where Selden could go with his patent. Henry agreed—and when Smith advised that the "Selden crowd" could put the Ford company out of business, Henry pointed a menacing finger and rejoindered, "Let them try it."

Betimes, the Model A Ford had to be tried. The very first pilot model had been wrecked on Mack Avenue sometime early that year, which might have proved disastrous save for the fact that Henry had never been satisfied with it anyway and had already improved it into a second car which served as the production prototype. Henry might have procrastinated further—as he had in the past—except that James Couzens, ledger in hand, enforced a get-the-money-first dictum which was applauded by Malcomson and the Dodge brothers. And so into production the Model A Ford went.

"The business went along almost as by magic." Ford would later recall. "The cars gained a reputation for standing up." Henry was partly right. In the fifteen months from mid-June of 1903 a very impressive 1700 cars were built and sold; the company was already a paying proposition. It was almost like magic—despite the fact that the Model A was a charming but not charmed car. Henry might even have thought it hexed at times. Flywheels came loose, water boiled in the radiator under the best of conditions (high gear, level road), the chains wore quickly, the oiling system was more flood than splash, bands slipped in the transmission. There ensued numerous shouting matches with the Dodge brothers—and it was back to the drawing board for Henry and company. The defects were remedied.

Paragon of automotive virtue though the Model A was not, it was nonetheless the way Henry Ford wanted to go. It was simple — the "Boss of the Road" ads appearing in *Collier's Weekly* and *Frank Leslie's Popular Monthly* extolling that a "Boy of fifteen can run it." Its two-cylinder (4 by 4) horizontal opposed engine developed a steady eight horsepower, and, set in a chassis measuring seventy-two inches, it weighed but 1250 pounds. "It would have been lighter had I known how to make it so," said Henry. Lightness to Henry Ford meant better engineering, improved efficiency and performance. That was in the Model A's favor. Henry had wanted to sell the car for $500 — and though he couldn't manage that, he concluded in ads that "its exceedingly reasonable price . . . places it within the reach of many thousands who could not think of paying the comparatively fabulous prices asked for most machines." Henry also commented to John Anderson in 1903: "The way to make automobiles is to make one automobile like another, to make them all alike, to make them come through the factory just alike." There was no question as to the road Henry Ford wanted to travel.

There were to be a couple of detours. The first was the Model B. The Model A had been improved into the AC and C, both ready late in 1904, and carrying slightly larger engines than the A (4¼ by 4¼) developing ten horsepower. Thirty miles an hour was the advertised top speed. Wheelbase had been increased to seventy-eight inches, and the price, too, to $800, subsequently to $850 and $950 for runabout and tonneau. But the weight complete remained at 1250 pounds. The principal difference between C and AC was the size and location of the gasoline tank: under the hood on the C, under the seat on the AC. Nothing startling there. But the Model B was something altogether different.

About the only specifications shared by the B and its brothers were a cone clutch, two-speed planetary transmission and gravity lubrication system. The B had shaft drive, not chain; rear hub drum brakes, not differential band; a three-cell storage battery, not dry cell. The prototype Model B, exhibited at the Automobile and Sportsman's Show in Detroit in February of 1904, was air cooled and had its flywheel mounted in front of the engine. (Flat "spokes" in the flywheel, set at an angle, served as fan blades.) The production version, however, reverted to water cooling and a standard flywheel at the rear with a separate fan in front. The engine was a vertical in-line four-cylinder affair of 4¼ by 5 inches displacing 318 cubic inches and developing 24 horsepower. It was set in a ninety-two-inch wheelbase chassis fitted with a touring car body and weighed 1700 pounds. It was capable of at least forty miles an hour. It would be priced at $2000. And Henry Ford didn't like it at all.

The Model B had been verily forced upon Henry — by Malcomson chiefly, who thought the company should claim its share of the moneyed market. (Ransom Olds was having similar problems with his directors at Lansing.) Ford thought otherwise, of course. Already he knew he had to do something about Malcomson. But first he had to do something about the Model B — like find a way to sell it.

With his fancy for the spectacular, he came up with an idea right away, one that would launch the Model B amid a flurry of publicity. Henry resuscitated the old Arrow — whose battered remains had somehow come to rest in Detroit after a racing accident at Milwaukee in 1903 — and overhauled its four-cylinder engine which he said was substantially identical to that of the forthcoming Model B. He renamed the car "999" — that name being considerably more famous than "Arrow," a logical enough move but one which would plague historians decades hence. Whatever it was called, however, it was with this car that Henry proposed to break the land speed record then held — he thought — by a Mors at 77.13 mph. Lake St. Clair would be the venue, January the month, and soon after New Year's of 1904 Henry, Clara, young Edsel and Spider Huff — among others — trekked to a resort hotel on Anchor Bay for the attempt. Snow was scraped and the ice cindered over a four-mile straight course. On January 9th Spider laid himself over the hulk of the Arrow-cum-999, Henry Ford settled himself into the driver's seat, and the two were off. Ice is most commonly thought of as smooth — but the stuff on Lake St. Clair certainly wasn't. It was an incredible ride—so rough and jolting that Henry's foot bounced off the throttle occasionally, but

---

*The Selden matter was a complicated affair, revolving around the gasoline automobile patent issued to George B. Selden in 1895. (He had initially made application in 1879, though he did not then build an automobile, nor would he until the court proceedings some two decades later.) Rights to the patent were accorded in 1899 by Selden to the Electric Vehicle Company which, when electric car sales began to wane, dusted off the patent and proceeded to demand royalties from every gasoline car manufacturer in America for each vehicle they produced, the Association of Licensed Automobile Manufacturers being set up to authorize licenses and collect royalties.

The Model F, 1905 / Henry Ford Museum

somehow Spider managed to substitute his when necessary. As Henry later recalled, "At every fissure the car leaped into the air. I never knew how it was coming down. When I wasn't in the air I was skidding." Henry ended the first run in a snowbank—there had, so the story goes, been a breakdown in communications. Spider, whose duties included puffing into the rubber hose leading to the gas tank, had devised a system with Henry. One kick from the driver meant "blow harder," two indicated "stop." Spider unfortunately forgot — and as the run was ending, the more Henry kicked him the harder he blew. Both survived the mistake, as did the car — and the three of them had run the straightaway mile in thirty-six seconds flat for 100 mph. There was a victory dinner that night at the Hotel Chesterfield. Everybody ate muskrat. Henry liked it.

The 100 mph run was unofficial — AAA timers not being present. They arrived three days later and another—official—run was staged, this one consuming 39.4 seconds for 91.37 mph for the straightaway mile. It was still a record, beating one (Arthur Duray's 84.73 mph in a Gobron-Brillie in France) of which Henry apparently wasn't even aware. The world land speed record belonged to Ford. It was widely promoted. Even some of Henry's new distributing agencies helped. In New York, John Wanamaker advertised: "Building the wonderful '999,' and driving it to this marvelous record, which is 6 3/5 seconds faster than any automobile ever went before, is merely the pasttime of Henry Ford. His real work—the business that engages all his brain, skill and experience—is the building of FORD MOTOR CARS —the best runabout machines that have yet been produced."

"That put Model B on the map," recalled Henry later, but he concluded it was not sufficient to make up for the car's high price. The Model B didn't sell especially well: One might suspect indeed that Henry Ford would have been disappointed if it had. Models C and AC were doing nicely—to his delight—as would the new Model F, introduced in February of 1905. At $1200 it bridged the price market between the C and B, although it was more akin to the former than the latter. A side entrance tonneau—the C remained rear entrance—and the first Ford with running boards, the Model F was powered by a 4½ by 4 two-cylinder opposed engine developing slightly more than 16 horsepower. Its wheels at 30 inches were two inches larger than the C's, two inches smaller than the B's. Its wheelbase at 84 inches and weight at 1400 pounds placed it midway between its companion models as well. Henry didn't have a lot to say about the F—significant in itself, although he did not object to it as strenuously as he did the B—but it is noteworthy that when thoughts turned to a redesign, he envisioned the new model as an improvement of the C *and* the F. The alphabetical designations missing between C and F, incidentally, were apparently assigned to experimental designs and engines conjured during this period, among them three- and five-cylinder rotary powerplants, both successfully operated, but discarded as impractical.

By early 1905 Ford operations had moved into a new plant on Piquette Avenue, ten times the size of the Mack Avenue facilities. Production perked along, Couzens informing reporters in April that the company was averaging twenty-five vehicles a day and now employed 300 men, while plant superintendent Al Andrich predicted a sixty-car-a-day output soon. Henry Ford was thinking even bigger; in May Detroit papers headlined "Plan Ten Thousand Autos at $400 Apiece," and when asked how, Henry responded, "it will take some time to figure out what we can do, and we do not care to say much until we know what the result will be." Looking around the spacious and new, but already

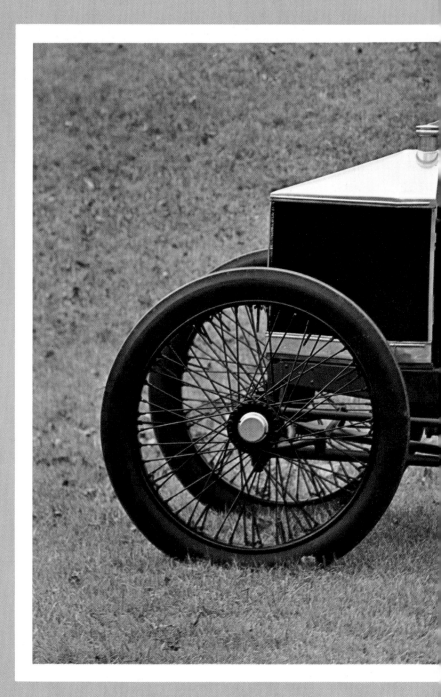

The 666 racer, 1906 / Henry Ford Museum

cluttered and somewhat disorganized plant, Henry and company concluded that there must be a better way to manufacture automobiles.

And still there was the problem of Malcomson. Disagreements between the Scotsman and Henry regarding the cars the company should be building continued unabated—and Henry concluded, with no apparent reluctance, that Malcomson would simply have to go. Seeing to it was as adventurous an undertaking as that winter's ride across Lake St. Clair. Malcomson had, however, contributed at least partly to his own impending demise by initially entrusting to his associate Couzens the running of the automobile business while he occupied himself chiefly with coal. When he decided to reverse these priorities and return Couzens to matters anthracitic or bituminous, Couzens simply said no — and Ford backed him up. Now Couzens and Ford were ready for the next step — both convinced that quantity manufacture of a light, inexpensive car should be the company's sole objective. To realize maximum prosperity from their plan, however, the firm would have to extend its manufacture to engines and running gear. To that end the two men devised the Ford Manufacturing Company, a separate entity incorporated on November 22nd, 1905, with a capital of $100,-000, just $50,000 actually being subscribed. Of the 5000 shares of stock issued, not one went to Malcomson. He was properly enraged, of course. As month passed month, however, and he realized the futility of his position (Ford profits could be carefully siphoned into the manufacturing company, leaving the parent company virtually broke), Malcomson conceded defeat and on July 12th, 1906, sold his interest in the Ford Motor Company to Henry for $175,000. Less than a year later Ford Motor and Ford Manufacturing would merge. John Gray had conveniently died, leaving the Ford Motor presidency open; Henry already had Ford Manufacturing's top spot. It had been nothing less than a revolution. The Ford Motor Company was now Henry's, to do with as he liked.

Of course, the Model K was already on the market. It was a big and beautiful car. Six cylinders, measuring 4½ by 4¼, cast singly, mounted vertically in line. Forty horsepower. A 114 (later 120) -inch wheelbase. Twenty-four hundred pounds in touring trim. Available too as a speedster with special springs, bucket seats and "a racing sport body designed to exclude eddy currents and air friction." Sixty miles an hour, guaranteed! Originally priced at $2500, it didn't make money. Raised to $2800, it still didn't. Henry wasn't fond of the Model K.

Introduced late in 1905, the Model K was Malcomson's last *coup de maître*. His insistence on its production can't really be faulted, since half the cars in America then were selling at or above the K's price tag: How could Malcomson know that Henry Ford was about to change all that? Still, Henry was stuck with the K — and, promotion of it in mind, he had set to building a racing version to break the now-oft-being-broken land speed record. Earlier he had hoped, the reader will recall, to garner profit-making prestige via record setting for the Model B. That hadn't worked. Perhaps it would with the Model K. Alas, initially, even the car didn't cooperate. In Florida in 1905 it broke its crankshaft while being warmed up in the Ormond Beach Garage. The new crank—it was supposed to have been turned from a solid steel billet—arrived welded together instead and promptly cracked at a weld. In the summer of 1905 Henry tried again — much to the distress of his associates who thought his life too valuable to be risked racing, and probably his wife, too, though characteristically Clara quietly demurred. At a beach race at Cape May, Henry's steed was slower than a Darracq, a Fiat and a Christie, and on the Atlantic City beach he was beaten by Walter Christie again in a two-man race.

The Model K, 1907 / Harrah's Automobile Collection

The Model N, 1906 / Henry Ford Museum

The Model R, 1907 / Henry Ford Museum

The Model S, 1908 / Henry Ford Museum

Undaunted, Henry took the racer — now improved from 60 to 100 horsepower, he said — to Ormond again in 1906, this time taking Frank Kulick with him. Kulick had spent much of the 1904 season winning races for Ford at such diverse locales as Grosse Pointe, Narragansett Park, Poughkeepsie and Chicago in a whimsical little 20 hp car — called "Baby Limited" by some — powered by a flat four comprised of two Model A Ford engines. Yonkers and the Empire City track provided its greatest victory, though, Kulick besting a huge 90 hp Fiat and a 60 hp Renault, lowering the one-mile record several times en route to a five-mile record of 62.4 mph. It was, the G. & J. Tire Company advertised, "as sensational a win in the automobile world, as T.R. in the political world." Maybe, Henry reasoned, Frank Kulick could do something with the troublesome six-cylinder racer.

Not at Ormond Beach, unfortunately. The first day's heat Frank missed because the clerk of the course forgot to tell him when it was, he lost to a Darracq in the next event and got stuck in the sand in another. A Stanley Steamer made the big record news that week; hardly anyone knew the Ford was even there. Better news followed the next year when Kulick, with Bert Lorimer, won a twenty-four-hour marathon at the Detroit Fairgrounds.

It was a remarkable achievement for both car and its drivers, especially Lorimer. He was entirely new to this game. As *The Motor World* pointed out, "Before the race he was a tester at the Ford works; after the twenty-four-hour grind he was a famous track driver." Lorimer had never raced before, indeed had never even been taken out to the fair grounds track; apparently he was pressed into service because no one else was available. His enthusiasm got the better of him—"Lorimer was always ready for a brush and took more chances on the turns than the old circuit chasers," *The Motor World* commented—and Henry was, for a while, beside himself with concern. He didn't trust the car. He had counselled Kulick, who started the event, to keep to a schedule of forty miles each for the first two hours, which Kulick observed to the letter, then increase the pace by five miles or so for the next two hours, which Kulick also did masterfully. At that point the K racer was lying third, and Lorimer took over. As *Motor Age* described it, "This was shortly before 3 o'clock in the morning and the small crowd which remained all night at the grounds was treated to some of the most daring driving ever seen on a mile track. Lorimer opened the Ford clear up on the long straights and speedily became a factor in the race. He took the curves high up on the banks and repeatedly negotiated miles in the even minute. Through the uncertain light of the gas lamps the car shot like a meteor, its exhaust an uninterrupted, flaming roar." When Kulick got back in the car, all restrictions were off. And the results were spectacular. At race conclusion, the Model K held the world's record for twenty-four hours, at 1135 miles and the very substantial margin of 309 miles over the old mark. The previous best track record for a day's racing had been 33.0 mph, the Model K now held it at 47.2 mph. Track records for intermediate distances and shorter times were smashed as well. As *The Automobile* said, "the six-cylinder Ford carried off all the honors."

But Henry was only mildly impressed—sufficiently so to take promotional advantage of the victory, but in a rather backhanded way. He offered to sell the winning car at the K's list price and "keep it in repair gratis for two years." Doubtless he didn't particularly want to have it around. Finally, the Ford six-cylinder racing saga came to an abrupt end that September, when Kulick, trying for an under-fifty-seconds mile record, nearly met his death at the Michigan State Fair. This car was apparently the one dubbed 666 by Henry Ford—unquestionably there

was more than one racer built—and it ended its competition life over an embankment, upside down. Henry wanted to bury it right there.

If the Model K was a disappointment to Henry, it was one tempered by the performance — in the marketplace — of its companion car: the Model N. Introduced with the K, it stole the big car's thunder. There were, after all, lots of big expensive cars on the market. But the sturdy little N was rather a novelty. It was priced at a mere $500 — and look what it had. A four-cylinder engine, first of all, the cylinders measuring 3¾ by 3⅜, cast in pairs, set in line and mounted up front under the hood. The cast iron flywheel with fan-shaped spoke (recalling the air cooled Model B) was mounted in front of the engine. Fifteen to eighteen horsepower was developed, for a speed in the 40 mph range. The wheelbase was eighty-four inches, the complete weight 800 pounds. In short, a lot of car for $500. *Cycle and Automobile Trade Journal* called it "distinctly the most important mechanical traction event of 1906."

The N was a solid hit. Ford couldn't make them fast enough, even after the price, of necessity, had climbed to $600. Dealers clamored for them and were duly provided; for every ten N's, however, they had to take one K — wily old Henry. Ford sales for 1904-1905 had totaled 1745 and the following season had dropped to 1599 as demand outstripped production on the N, the reverse being true for the K. But for 1906-1907 they soared to 8423. And the N was given a brother, in response to dealer requests. The Model R, announced in February of 1907, was described by the company, frankly and accurately, as "a car of more pretentious appearance." It was simply a gussied-up N with "more frills and fussings, more brass trimmings." All this added 300 pounds to the car's weight and $150 to its price. The 2500 R's built were virtually sold out by September of 1907 — and the company said it was "too late to build more." Ergo the Model S: a composite, the company insisted, of the N and the R, and priced at $700, a roadster version following at $750. Some 6398 Models N and S would be sold the following season.

Henry had come a long way from that Christmas Eve engine demonstration in Clara's kitchen sink. He had enjoyed through the lean years the unrelenting faith and confidence of his wife; at every successive critical juncture, and as he grew more successful, he had garnered the financial backing of prominent and substantial businessmen who, by and large, also believed in him. That, combined with a considerable amount of talent and vision, provides sufficient hindsight for us to conclude today that he couldn't have missed.

By now Henry was planning new facilities at Highland Park. And by now, too, he had brought into his employ a Danish-born, gifted and moody pattern maker by the name of Charles E. Sorensen and a Vermonter named Walter E. Flanders whose experience in machine tools, factory production set-up and management loomed as large as he did. It was Childe Harold Wills who suggested the recruitment of Joseph Galamb, a brilliant Hungarian engineer trained in the automobile plants of Germany. And it was Henry himself who discovered the talents and ingenuity of C.J. ("Jimmy") Smith, a young machinist already working for Ford who would, Henry thought, prove useful.

One day during the winter of 1906-1907, Henry Ford took Charles Sorensen to the third floor of the Piquette plant and, pointing to an unoccupied area, asked that a room be put there "with a door . . . big enough to run a car in and out." The door was to have a lock, and regarding what was to come out, Henry told a reporter in October only that he hoped it would be "in the nature of forked lightning." It was a rare example of Henry Ford understatement.

PART TWO:
Model T

America was perhaps ready for the automobile, but the extent of the country's preparedness remains debatable. True, automobile registrations by 1907 passed the 140,000 mark, an impressive leap from the turn of the century figure of 8000. Still, an opinion poll in 1903 had indicated that a mere five percent of Americans favored the automobile, enraged non-owners of the vehicle continued a vociferous dissent (one suggesting intervention by the Humane Society), and publications like the *North American Review* pointed out ominously in 1906 that automobiles had killed more citizens in the five months previous than had perished in the Spanish American War. (How sadly contemporary that sounds.) There were the vigilante rear-guard efforts of those wily farmers near Sacramento, California, who dredged ditches across several roads and succeeded in trapping thirteen cars, and recourse to constitutionally-approved action in those proposals to curtail or eliminate the motorized beast which were offered at frequent intervals to municipal and state governing bodies across the country. Though more and more automobiles were appearing on American roads, it was evident that many Americans remained to be convinced of the vehicle's real widespread utility—at least to the extent that Henry Ford was about to convince them. A consumer revolt didn't bring forth the Model T; Henry Ford did. And he knew exactly what he was doing. He was providing America with an automobile he knew it wanted, even if America itself wasn't altogether sure.

Among all the good ideas that have blossomed forth during the Mechanical Age, Henry's Model T must remain in the first rank. He had been thinking about it for a half decade previous to 1908, and wouldn't consider another for almost two decades thereafter, and then only reluctantly. The Model T he perceived as the universal car, one which once built would forever answer the personal transportation needs of America. And if he miscalculated on that particular, its

significance pales in the light of what he accomplished. The Model T, most scholars agree, brought about a revolution in the mode of American life. Defining the automobile in a practical sense as an efficient and economical means of transport of wide application and availability, it must be viewed, historically, as the most important car ever built. It remains among the most endearing. A unique automobile it is that cannot be compared with any other. The Model T Ford stands quite alone.

Several factors made possible Henry's car for the people. Among them was vanadium steel, a piece of which Henry had picked up from a wrecked French racer in Palm Beach in 1905, the superior qualities of which had prompted Henry's first attempt as an author (an article on its uses for *Harper's Weekly* in 1907), and the utilization of which throughout the Model T would make for the not-unduly-exaggerated claim that the Ford was the strongest built car in the world. Another factor was the manner in which the Ford Model T would be manufactured, more of which later. Still another was the design of the Model T itself, providing lightness with durability (vanadium steel playing its important role here) *and* power *and* masterful simplicity — a combination altogether new for a car whose price would make it available to legions of would-be automobilists hitherto neglected.

Henry Ford did not design the Model T alone, of course—though every piece of it reflected his thinking. As we have seen, he had already gathered around him a coterie of men who would translate thoughts into the tangible, brainstorms into the workable. So attuned was Charles Sorensen that after a time he didn't even bother awaiting blueprints; simply hearing an idea from Henry was sufficient go-ahead for him to make a pattern and cast it. In the little twelve-by-fifteen-foot room Ford had cordoned off for the project, Joseph Galamb would spend months

HENRY AND LIZZIE-
AMERICA
IS PUT ON WHEELS

of post-sundown days at work, as would Childe Harold Wills, assigned initially to metallurgical development, Jimmy Smith and the others. But among all the residents of the car's incubation chamber, Henry Ford was the most dominant.

Dominating the room was a blackboard whereon design ideas were drawn in full scale and photographed—and a rocking chair belonging to Henry's mother which he had brought there for good luck. The rocking chair faced the blackboard; one would doubt that it was ever occupied by other than Henry. He was there every day, sometimes at seven or eight at night, other times earlier. As Jimmy Smith recalled, "He brought ideas to us. First he would think the thing up, then he would have [the draftsmen] draw it up, and then we would make it up." There was probably more give and take in the project than that suggests, though even Galamb subsequently insisted that Ford's ideas were predominant throughout. Apparently there was no friction between the boss and his men. The relationship between them was cordial—and solid. As George Brown, another Ford employee, later related, "He'd never say, 'I *want* this done!' He'd say, 'I wonder if we can do it. I wonder.' Well, the men would just break their necks to see if they could do it. They knew what he wanted." From all available accounts of men who were there, it appears that Henry got his way through humble persuasion, not hardheaded coercion. And for those who recall Henry only as the Obstinate, the Recalcitrant, the Unyielding—it's pleasant, and revealing, to reflect upon those obviously happy months when the Model T was born.

Make no mistake about it, the Model T was exactly what Henry Ford wanted, every inch of it. Once it was completed, Henry was through with experimenting. On that glorious day when the Model T was finally brought down from the third floor for its first test run, Henry's enthusiasm almost overwhelmed him — and everyone else. Perhaps too excited to drive the car himself, he asked associate

George Holley to take him downtown. The pair coursed the streets of Detroit; Henry, drinking in the sweetness of revenge, made sure that the trek took him past the offices of Alexander Malcomson. Returning home, he gave everyone within striking distance "a kick in the pants" or a "punch in the shoulders." "Well," he said, "I guess we've got started." George Brown also recalled his saying with regard to the T's production potential, "I wonder if we'll get up to number ten." Henry was only kidding.

It would have required a man with but a thimbleful of its creator's engineering genius to realize at once that Henry Ford had come up with a winner. It wasn't a perfect car by any means — though Henry obviously thought it was — but what it was was close enough to the average man's motoring ideal in those days to render its shortcomings trifling.

The company itself probably said it best in one of the early brochures: "The Ford is a better car, not because it costs less, but because it is worth more." For $850, which was the T's initial price tag, it was quite a car. One feels somewhat loath to describe it, it is part of the car's mystique perhaps to assume that virtually every American knows the Model T as well or better than the car he is now driving. As the late John Steinbeck recalled regarding the T's transmission, two generations of Americans knew more about "the planetary system of gears than the solar system of stars." Still, for those whose interests lie in the heavens or the non-motorized areas of the earth, a few words.

The T's engine was a four-cylinder side valve affair with bore/stroke dimensions of 3¾ by 4 inches for a displacement of 176.7 cubic inches (2.9 liters), providing for 20 bhp (and 65 lb/ft of torque) at 1600 rpm. The cylinders, with their water jackets, were cast en bloc, and integrated with the upper half of the crankcase — an exemplary piece of foundry work, by the way. The cylinder head was a separate casting and was easily detachable, leaving valves and pistons conveniently exposed for maintenance work, an idea scoffed at initially by Ford's rivals (wouldn't it leak?) but adopted by them (no, it wouldn't) in the years following. Built in unit with the engine was the transmission, the flywheel housing and the universal joint — a neat package. Ignition was via a low tension magneto incorporated in the flywheel — a familiar practice in Europe but rather innovative for the United States. Lubrication was by what one reporter called "a peculiar splash system" — actually a combination gravity and splash which was ingenuous but had the saving grace of being absolutely adequate to its task. The first T's featured centrifugal water pumps, soon replaced by a simpler thermosyphon system.

The chassis was light, strong (who can recall a broken T chassis?) and of blessed simplicity. Three-point suspension was used throughout: engine, front and rear axle; two springs sufficed, both semi-elliptics mounted crosswise directly over the axles. The arrangement for stopping the first Model T's comprised two pedals and two levers, the wheel brake and reverse band actuated by individual hand controls, but this system was abandoned by late February of 1909 in favor of what became probably the three most famous pedals in the world. Equally acclaimed — sometimes defamed — was the two-speed planetary transmission, not a new idea itself but improved on the T, with the entire system, main clutch and footbrake enclosed and running in oil — and the gear change operation being foot controlled, a pleasantly pragmatic and simple idea. Journalists of the day also noted that the noise in low or reverse of previous planetary transmissions had been eliminated by the T's increased size of the externally driven gears, this producing "the same quiet purring sound whether the car is running fast or slow, forward or backward." One must allow for a certain disparity regarding the pleasure quotient of decibel levels in those days and these.

Interestingly, as proud as Henry was of the planetary transmission, he did allow the word to be spread initially that it was "almost unnecessary" — this because of the very favorable power-to-weight ratio of the car. The first T's weighed in at about 1200 pounds — subsequently they got a little heavier — and the engine, as mentioned, produced twenty horses. Nothing comparable had ever previously been available in such an attractively priced car. The wheelbase was 100 inches, track fifty-six and chassis length 128. Bodies were wood (the few sheet aluminum variations presumably being experimental). Though not a rainbow of colors by any means, the first T's could be had painted in either black, red, green, pearl or French gray.

On March 18th, 1908, an advance catalogue about the T was sent to Ford dealers. That might have been a mistake. Ford was producing the Model S at the time, and in April in the *Ford Times* the company felt compelled to remind their dealers that it was "the nobbiest little car offered this year," it was a good seller and "we simply mention this because some of the Agents seem to be waiting for something to turn up instead of hustling to sell what they can secure deliveries on and what the public is anxious to buy." The smart Ford dealers probably hid the advance brochure, went about the business of selling the S and waited for the T to turn up. It did, at the branch managers meeting in Detroit held from September 14th through the 17th. All were impressed. The first factory-built T was completed on September 24th; and Henry commandeered it for a hunting trip in northern Wisconsin. Eight more T's were built in October, and interestingly the entire lot was shipped to Europe (Ford's overseas representatives were obviously zealous) to be shown at the Olympia (London) and Paris shows in November. The press reaction in both cities was restrained, *The Autocar*, for example, merely citing Ford together with Cadillac as "two noble exponents of the small car." Some 253 orders were taken at Olympia.

The Model T was not to be officially exhibited in the United States until the last day of December at Grand Central Palace in New York, but already the car was a sensation. The announcement ad for the T had appeared in *The Saturday Evening Post* on October 3rd, a Friday; as the *Ford Times* exulted a week and a half later, "Saturday's mail brought nearly one thousand inquiries. Monday's response swamped our mail clerks and by Tuesday night the office was well nigh inundated." The Model T Ford had really got started.

Almost as quickly had come the somewhat startling announcement that the new car would be the company's only model, the chassis identical for runabout, touring car, town car and delivery car alike. That proposition was met with considerable skepticism in the industry and the press — and had earlier been greeted with disfavor by some members of the Ford hierarchy. Production man Walter Flanders had been among them, and he had left the company on April 15th, 1908, upon the receipt of a tempting offer from the Wayne Automobile Company, which, with William A. Metzger and Barney F. Everitt, he quickly converted into the E-M-F Company. Interestingly, in January of 1909, in an interview in *Scientific American* he proffered his notions regarding the new E-M-F, a car worth more than $2500 but which with his manufacturing methods could be produced to sell for half that: "There are at least half a million people in the United States today who can afford a $1250 car," he concluded brightly. Henry, of course, was thinking bigger than that.

In mid-1909, however, the Ford company had to advise dealers not to "send in

1909 Tourabout / Owner: Charles Bowers

1909 New York-Seattle Racer / Henry Ford Museum

1910 Super T, 999 II / Henry Ford Museum

1910 Torpedo Runabout / Owner: Robert Dean (formerly Paul Tusek)

any more orders until advised by this office." Henry had continued to be deluged with them, he could build only 18,257 T's during 1909, and he began taking steps to assure that production in the future would keep pace with demand. The first problem met was the wasteful inefficiency in freighting fully-assembled cars in quantity to distances several thousand miles from Detroit. By the summer of 1909 the company had decided to establish branch assembly plants to which as many as seven knocked-down T's could be shipped in a single ordinary box car (alleviating the expense of special freight cars) and duly put together for distribution to dealers in the outlying region. It was a massive project, one which would be overseen by a former Danish bicycle mechanic whom Henry Ford had discovered in the John R. Keim Mills in Buffalo, a pressed steel manufacturing company that was initially a Ford supplier and ultimately purchased by Ford. He was William S. Knudsen.

Apparently it was in the fall of 1909 that William Durant, who had been happily gathering companies under the umbrella of a new firm called General Motors (Buick, Olds, Oakland, Cadillac) approached Henry Ford acquisitively. Sure, responded Henry, you can buy the Ford Motor Company — for eight million dollars . . . cash. Durant couldn't come up with that, and the deal fell through. Benjamin Briscoe had also entertained Durantian thoughts about adding Ford to his United States Motor Company, and Henry offered the same proposition. One can only assume that Henry's response in both cases was in the nature of rib-tickling. His sense of humor was often piquant, and one can imagine him enjoying a good laugh with Jim Couzens while the would-be purchasers scurried haplessly to procure the sums that Henry was convinced were simply impossible for them to get. What self-respecting banker in those days would finance in cold and considerable cash such a still speculative proposition as an automobile company? None, as it turned out.

By now, however, Henry could not take the Selden matter so lightly. Despite the rebuff from the A.L.A.M. in 1903, he had decided to build his cars anyway — without a license — as a number of other manufacturers had. The A.L.A.M. then filed suit for patent infringement — and Henry prepared to do battle. About the time of the Durant overtures to him — on September 15th, 1909 — the courts had ruled in favor of the complainants, acknowledging George Selden as the inventor of the automobile and his patent holders as legally entitled to royalties. But Henry wasn't about to give up, though other erstwhile recalcitrants — William Durant among them — quickly applied for licenses and proceeded to submit back royalties. Instead, Henry went to the Court of Appeals, and fought, and the court's ruling of January 9th, 1911, affirming that the patent was indeed valid but only as it applied to automobiles using Selden's Brayton-type two-cycle engine (which had long since been abandoned in automobile design), effectively quashed its promoters' dreams of monopoly in the automobile industry, and the A.L.A.M. along with it. Henry Ford emerged from the encounter as a genuine folk hero — an appealing maverick, a gutsy little fighter who had defied "the Trust" and won. As far as Henry was concerned, it had provided terrific advertising for the Model T.

Henry had a way of preferring the news columns to the display ad as a vehicle for promoting his product, his company and—not incidentally — himself. He and his company were becoming good copy, and the press bristled with the news. These random headlines from automobile publications of the day tell the company story as it was unfolding: "Ford Opening New Plant" (October 1910); "Ford Reduces Prices" (November 1910); "Ford Company Plans Large Out-

1911 Touring Car / Owner: Ray Nelson

1911 Town Car / Owner: Richard E. Williams

44

1912 Speedster / Formerly Walter Beatty

1913 Closed Cab Pick-Up / Owner: John M. Dunne

put" (October 1911); "Ford Co. Purchases Chicago Block" (August 1912); "Ford Co. Has Surplus of $14,745,095" (January 1913).

Nor was Henry wasting any time in providing similar headlines for the Model T itself. He had decided to race again — for a while. A golden opportunity had been presented him by Robert Guggenheim. To promote the Alaska-Yukon-Pacific Exposition in Seattle, the young magnate had devised the idea of a coast-to-coast run from New York to that Washington city to take place the summer of 1909. Entries had originally comprised thirty-five, dwindled to fourteen, and finally to six. This may have been the result of opposition to the race by the A.L.A.M.; the Selden patent suit was then broiling, and Ford's enthusiasm for the race might have discouraged the licensed manufacturers. Moreover, the Automobile Club of America's oft-changed rules for the contest were both exacting and confusing, and that may have discouraged others. So might have Henry's audacity. He deftly garnered press notices by challenging any manufacturer to bet any amount of money that his car could beat a Ford. There were no takers. So on June 1st, as President Taft in the White House pressed the golden telegraph key to open the exposition, Mayor George McClellan in New York simultaneously fired a gold-plated pistol from the steps of City Hall — and five cars were off (two Model T's, a 48 hp Acme, a 45 hp Shawmut and a 50 hp Itala). The sixth car, a Stearns, started from City Hall five days later and quit twenty-four miles after that.

Less than ten percent of the 4106 miles of road traversed in the contest were "improved" (which at that time probably meant passable in wet weather), and that bald fact is sufficient to indicate the rigors of the journey. Rather than offer a recital of the gumbo, the quicksand, the unfordable streams, the sand storms, the hail storms, the four-foot snowdrifts — all of which are probably better imagined anyway — it might suffice to say only that Ford No. 2 (driven by Bert Scott and Jimmy Smith) was first to arrive in Seattle, on June 23rd, twenty-two days and fifty-five minutes from New York's City Hall, followed by the Shawmut seventeen hours later, Ford No. 1 (driven by Frank Kulick and H. B. Harper) on June 25th, and the Acme on June 29th. The Itala arrived in Seattle via freight car, having given up the chase in Cheyenne, Wyoming.

Had not nature provided enough obstacles for the trek, the reminiscences of the participants revealed a number of others. Ford No. 2 was almost destroyed by fire: "While filling with gasoline, some sport with less sense than is usually allotted even to those we coop up in asylums for the weak-minded struck a match on the side of the tank." Ford No. 1 was several times hopelessly lost with the help of navigators acquired along the way: "At Wallula we picked up another bone-headed specimen for a pilot. This road juggler lost us in what is known as the Horse Heaven Country, and when we should have been in Prosser, Washington, we were in Mottinger. Any jury in the land would have brought in a verdict of justifiable homicide if we had followed our inclination in regard to the excess baggage that had hired out as pilot to us." The Ford drivers, who obviously had suffered nature gladly, were not as happy to do likewise with fools. One can understand their intemperance.

All obstacles notwithstanding, a Ford had won — and the papers were full of the news. Henry had delighted himself every day of the trek with the journalistic accounts, though some of the more sensational might have vexed him a bit (". . . often keeping a dangerous, foolhardy, daredeviltrous clip of 40 to 50 miles per hour the autos . . . tore into Toledo last night . . ." reported the *Toledo Blade*.) And now in Seattle Robert Guggenheim awarded the trophy saying, "I believe Mr. Ford has the solution of the popular automobile" — his remarks, of course, being liberally quoted throughout the country. Henry helped too with a booklet entitled "The Story of the Race" distributed in the tens of thousands to dealers, abetted by countless advertisements announcing that duplicates of the winning car could be seen — and ordered — in any Ford showroom: "It's the one reliable car that does not require a $10,000 income to buy, a $5,000 bank account to run and a college course in engineering to keep in order."

As postscript it should be added that subsequent to the race there was a claim that the winning Ford car had changed its engine for part of the run in violation of the rules, and the Shawmut was the true victor. This was denied at the time — and later — by Scott, and the race committee's seals affixed in New York were still on the car's engine in Seattle. It hardly mattered anyway. The word was already out — and the word was that the Ford was a winner.

In 1910 a stripped Model T, with Frank Kulick at the helm, raced an iceboat across Lake St. Clair, and won — then Kulick went on to more serious dirt track competition in the East, winning three firsts in a day at Brighton Beach and being victorious twice in races in Syracuse, New York.

Nineteen eleven was even better. After a remarkable Mardi Gras race meeting performance in New Orleans (five firsts and two seconds amid a field of cars all of which advertised horsepower in excess of the T's), car and Kulick confined themselves generally to the Midwest — in and around Chicago (setting a new record at the Algonquin Hill Climb) and in Milwaukee contests (two days, three firsts). And at the Detroit Fairgrounds on September 26th, after winning two preliminary events in a stripped T, Kulick rolled out a Super T variation with a prow-shaped radiator and a stout engine which probably shared only its number of cylinders with that of the stock Model T. With this little car Kulick proposed to better Bob Burman and his acclaimed Blitzen Benz, both of whom were there to see that upstart Kulick didn't do it. But he did. The Super T put up a lap in 50 seconds flat, Burman's best was 51.4. Eight thousand watched the spectacle, including Henry Ford who, as had happened on occasion during his earlier racing years, was less impressed with the excitement of the competition than its dangers — and at the conclusion of the event he pressed a thousand-dollar bill into Kulick's hand "to quit racing." Apparently he had second thoughts a few months later, because Kulick and the Super T (now renamed 999 II) were on Lake St. Clair in early 1912, with Henry's blessing, for sprints across the ice at 103.4 mph with mechanic (and 107.8 mph sans companion), breaking Henry's old ice record of 1904. Then in the summer Kulick and a stripped stock T took the Algonquin Hill Climb again in a performance so embarrassing to heavy-car builders that they threatened to boycott the contest the following year unless Kulick and his car were disqualified. This would prove unnecessary because by that time the Ford Motor Company had disavowed racing altogether.

There were many reasons for this, one of them exemplified by Ford's ill-fated attempt to run a revised 999 II in the 1913 Indianapolis 500. Officials had decreed the car could compete only with the addition of 1000 pounds in order to meet the minimum weight limit. "We're building race cars, not trucks," Henry told them — and promptly forgot about the whole thing.

The T's problem — so Henry said — was that it was discriminated against in events requiring competitors to conform to the A.A.A.'s weight or price classifications. The T was infinitely superior to anything in its class — and Henry's objectives were to prove it superior as well to heavier and more expensive cars. This the rules did not always allow. Giving the Model T dead weight or an inflated price to qualify were anathema to Ford, and consequently he just quit. By 1913, too, he was well enough involved in the manufacturing revolution taking place in his factory, was probably anticipating a public outcry against racing because of the fatalities in recent years (Syracuse, Milwaukee) and even no doubt was considering the bad publicity that might accrue should the Model T become a loser (as well it might have in those years of rather rapid technological advances.) Besides there were all those glorious press clippings about Kulick's exploits, how he "gobbled up" the competition, "showed his dust" to the foe, "had things all his own way"—and the various mentions of how the "little car made an excellent showing against the high powered foreigner." Getting out while still ahead looked to be a most attractive proposition.

The Model T scarcely needed publicizing any longer anyway. She (and here's one car whose gender has seldom been in doubt) had already become an international celebrity. Representatives of the Russian War Department had watched her win a race in 1912 sponsored by the Automobile Club of Moscow. Australians had thrilled to her conquering "The Gluepots" en route to a victory in the Sydney-to-Melbourne Reliability Contest of 1913. She had been the first to scale Scotland's Ben Nevis, to climb the Tambourine in Australia, the Andes in South America; she dared to cross the Gobi in Mongolia, to descend to the depths of the Grand Canyon and to climb courthouse or capitol steps across the breadth of America. She appeared in remote areas of the world where automobiles had never before been seen. She was discovered to be an admirable substitute for dog sleds in the Klondike, a better tiger-chasing device than drums in Korea, and a most efficient mode by which "home-hunters" could scout for suitable sites to settle in the empty wilds of Florida. (The company exampled this last exploit as "but another illustration of Ford's service on civilization's edges.")

Although the Model T Ford could count among her fans a modest number of royal owners (two Russian grand dukes, no less than nineteen princes), and the Ford company enticed such celebrities as Eddie Foy, Billie Burke and Henrietta Crossman to sit beguilingly behind her steering wheel for publicity photos, the Model T was not really at ease amid such grandeur. Before the First World War Ford abandoned what had been at best a lukewarm effort to give the T snob appeal, and thereafter her celebrity status was more aptly achieved with the Keystone Cops, Charlie Chaplin, Marie Dressler and Ben Turpin in films in which she was a star in her own right.

All this was ephemeral, of course. More important than the Model T herself was what she accomplished. America was a vastly different place after the Tin Lizzie's nineteen-year drive across the land. Quantitatively her impact perhaps can never be absolutely measured; yet even today she is acceded by virtually all to be one of the major social forces during two decades of American history. She was the Great Liberator, freeing rural America from the monotony and isolation of geography, demonstrating in the cities by her vast numbers the utility of automotive transport for business and public service. And, as social historian Frederick Lewis Allen has pointed out, by providing "a suitable place for misconduct" she took a chip out of "one of the cornerstones of American morality." The Model T brought Americans — as well as America — closer together. One can scarcely imagine an area of life in those days in which she did not exert some considerable influence.

All this might lead one to conclude that the altogether remarkable Model T was flawless. Not true. She might best be described as the imperfect ideal. Indeed her flawed character may have rekindled in America the pioneer spirit lost with the passing of the frontier — and for that we should look kindly upon every rattle in her bones. A Model T Ford brought out the ingenuity of its owner as much as crossing the plains in a Conestoga had taxed the resourcefulness of the homesteader.

Let it be said straightaway that the Ford Motor Company was convinced the T would seldom herself necessitate any remedial action, and they said so quite nicely. "We may as well admit first as last that most of our motor car troubles are due to our own neglect or mistreatment . . . " noted one company booklet. But Lizzie helped. Take starting, for instance. She was a temptress. John Steinbeck fondly recalled that she knew exactly the number of spins of the crank he would endure before he would kick in her radiator — and she always started on the last one. And Floyd Clymer remembered the sweet sound — "like a thresher trimming the nap off an acre of barbed wire" — when Lizzie began to hit on two, three, then four cylinders. Applying boiling water or a blowtorch (or in its absence a lighted gasoline-soaked rag or corncob) to the intake manifold was generally sufficient to start her on a cold morning. If water, blowtorch or its substitute weren't handy, one might try jacking up one of the rear wheels, releasing the handbrake and then cranking—or removing the spark plugs, rushing to the kitchen stove, heating the plugs to red hot, rushing back and screwing them back in (an awkward business with thick gloves and impossible without). But once the Model T was brought to life, she wanted to move, regardless of whether the owner had made it to the driver's seat. Her handbrake was frequently ineffectual, and as one Midwest owner reminisced, she "advanced on you the instant the first explosion occurred." Depending on his and the T's whereabouts at the time, the owner might find himself being not-so-gently pressed against his garage wall, or on the offensive in pursuit of the runaway.

In fine fettle the Model T was a joy to drive — and a wonder. Of her planetary transmission, "half metaphysics, half sheer friction," Lee Strout White wrote that "any car which was capable of going from forward into reverse without any perceptible mechanical hiatus was bound to be a mighty challenging thing to the human imagination." John Keats concluded that it took a year's practice before an owner conquered the gears and "could get into high without bounding down the road, looking like a frog with St. Vitus' dance and sounding like a canning factory with something wrong with it." There were the occasional annoyances to an afternoon's outing, like any stop for gas — the fuel tank was under the front seat and everybody had to be uprooted for refueling. The gravity fuel feed system sometimes meant that on very steep grades the T's engine might be starved. The simple solution: reversing up hills. One got the knack of that after a while. Sometimes Lizzie offered a choice of conditions under which to drive. The electric lights (fitted in 1915) were driven off the low-tension magneto; the faster the engine rotated, the more luminescent the path ahead. An owner thus frequently found that nighttime driving in low gear was preferable to high and a road seen only in flickers.

Still one would be hard put to quarrel with the Model T's roadworthiness. The farmer who wrote the Ford company insisting that a speedometer would be redundant on his T because "When I go 5 miles an hour . . . the fenders rattle; when I go 15 miles an hour my false teeth drop out; and when I go 25 miles an hour the transmission drops off" was only displaying that splendid good humor that marked the legions of T owners. Jokes about her became a national institution. Shimmy though she might; heave, rattle and wheeze, the Model T was a very happy car on the road. Certainly not less so were her passengers.

1913 Touring Car / Henry Ford Museum

1913 Runabout / Owner: Richard E. Williams

1915 Coupelet / Owner: Richard E. Williams

1919 Ford-Ames Dirt Track Racer / Leslie R. Henry

"Drive a horse ten thousand miles day in and day out — and you'll need a new horse. The Ford will need but new tires . . ." exclaimed the Ford company. Allowing for promotional hyperbole, one must conclude that whatever the Ford might need in addition to that was readily available. The Model T was probably the most fixable car ever built, limited only by the imagination of her owner. A screwdriver, a monkey wrench, baling wire, fishline, stove pipe, waxed twine; a paper clip might be just the thing, a bent nail would do wonders, and, oh, the uses of chewing gum. There's that marvelous story from 1916 of the Model T that broke down, fortuitously, in front of a junk shop. Her owner hopped out, ran in, spent thirty cents on a bedspring, a broken fly swatter, a piece of garden hose and assorted odds and ends, ran back, lifted the hood, fitted the newly-bought material, cranked the motor and drove off — whereupon the shop owner took down his "Junk of All Kinds" sign and replaced it with one reading "Ford Parts and Accessories." It didn't happen really, but one wishes it had.

No matter. The Model T was as fascinating in fact as in fiction. One did not own her, one was involved. She was an individual, she was skittish, she was eccentric, she was unpredictable. If the leaves split in her springs, she might list to port — then again she might list to starboard. No two Lizzies were alike (a Model T owner will never be convinced otherwise, and rightly so); every one was different — and yet they were all the same. . . .

The mass production of automobiles had its birth at Highland Park in August, 1913. Its conception at Ford, however, dated back five years, to the waning months of the Models N and S when a 100-units-per-day production schedule was maintained at the Piquette plant. There standardization of parts combined with simplification of product, an orderly floor plan with masterful, sequential positioning of machines, materials and men had provided several elements integral to the mass production concept. (Some of Ford's competitors had these too.) A hundred cars a day could be easily built that way. But Henry Ford was thinking much bigger. What was needed to build thousands was *movement,* continuous and carefully timed movement throughout the production procedure. Henry, together with P. E. Martin (a burly French Canadian who had been with Ford since 1904) and Sorensen had recognized its importance at Piquette, but it was not until the move to the newer and larger Highland Park plant in 1910 that the idea could be given full attention and the awkward beginnings made.

"The idea came in a general way from the overhead trolley that the Chicago packers use in dressing beef," Henry later reminisced, that being the suggestion of Ford foreman William C. Klann. First Model T radiator parts were conveyor-carried to assemblers. With that the ever cost-conscious James Couzens, in Henry's words, went "on the warpath." But, Henry advised Sorensen, "don't take him too seriously." Sorensen didn't, but he did manage to convince Couzens that scientific management had not gone mad, and that spending now in this case would result in saving later. Couzens was mollified. More and more Ford parts began to move — and finally the assembly line itself, first for the magneto, then the engine, then the transmission. Then more Ford men — Clarence W. Avery among them — joined in with the problem of final assembly. In August 1913, the chassis assembly line moved, experimentally via an electric motor with capstan and a heavy rope. In operation on October 7th, now by rope and windlass, the Ford men found that man hours per chassis had decreased from twelve and a half to less than six! With refinements (including an endless chain, rope being inadequate to the task), chassis time was cut to one hour thirty-three minutes by January of 1913. There were the occasional lapses, of course. William Klann recalled that "we had our chain going and some fellow forgot to open up the door, where [the chassis] go out and we buckled up three [of them]." That happened only once. In 1914 Ford produced more than 300,000 Model T's, while the rest of the American industry was putting together about a hundred thousand less. And that was only the beginning. An exultant Sorensen was heard to say that they could build as many as they wanted to, all they had to do was "speed up the line. Just make the belt run faster." He was exaggerating, but only a little.

Henry might have been exaggerating too when he said in 1912 there would be no changes in his Model T because it could not be improved. That declaration could have been prompted by his discovery that year, upon return from a trip to Europe, of an all-new Model T that Wills and his associates had designed in his absence. So angry was he that he had the car taken out into the street and personally smashed it to pieces. No, there definitely would be no new Model T. But the Model T they had would not remain absolutely untouched. Engineering changes were minimal, such refinements as occasioned by common sense (the replacement of the troublesome front axle adjustable ball bearings by roller bearings, for example, or the addition of a removable connecting rod pan to eliminate the annoyance of having to remove the entire engine to adjust rod bearings), or by efforts to reduce cost or speed up production. Outward changes in the T reflected this same thinking, particularly, of course, the famous "any color so long as it's black" policy instituted in 1914, this because *only* black Japan enamel would dry as fast as Fords were being built on the moving assembly line. A tentative step in that direction had been made two years earlier with the replacement of brass for such items as windshield mountings, lamps, horn and steering wheel spokes by black-painted steel. And the year following — 1915 — saw the cherrywood dash give way to a curved steel cowl; that year, too, brought a curve to the rear fenders and electric lights replacing the previous acetylenes. Nineteen thirteen had seen front doors affixed to the touring car; the driver's side, however, was a cleverly embossed, non-opening dummy, just about the only nonfunctional aspect of the T — why should it open, Henry probably thought, when the handbrake obstructed the doorway and the driver could just as easily slide across the seat to get out. Since 1911 the car was sheet steel covering a wooden frame. Commensurate with T modifications were the annual changes in price — downward: in 1914, $490; in 1915, $440. The T was now selling for just about half what it had when first introduced.

There were 7000 dealers in the Ford harness in 1914, all abiding by the rigorous strictures the company laid down for them. They could handle Ford cars only, had to keep meticulous showrooms, adequate stocks of parts and be ever on the alert to give immediate assistance to any T owner requiring it. The company furnished them price lists of parts for their customers — most unusual, parts lists in those days were seldom priced — and also Ford agents to teach them how to best handle parts stocks and do repair work. Ford's biggest problem then remained whom to allow in among the numberless applicants — mayors, congressmen and ex-governors among them — who were sure they were the personification of the "live wide-awake hustlers" the company demanded. Their anxiousness to please was understandable. In exchange for heavy supervision the Ford dealers were given a virtual get-rich-quick-and-then-get-richer guarantee. What could stop the Model T? Nothing, it seemed, absolutely nothing. The Ford dealers were a disciplined but happy lot.

It was on January 5th, 1914, that Henry Ford made his workers happy too. Although his presence in the factory was by no means an infrequent occurrence,

1916 Chemical Hose Truck / Owner: Allan C. Myers

1919 Sedan / Henry Ford Museum

1920 Chemical Hose Truck, fire equipment by American LaFrance
Long Island Automotive Museum

1920 Closed Cab Pick-Up, "The Little Red Truck" / Owner: George Norton

the days of Henry's back-slapping, first-name intimacy with his men were long gone. There were simply too many of them now, nearly 15,000 — quite a jump from the 450 of the T's introductory year. At that time a general excitement had filled the Ford plant, as an ebullient Henry trekked through the shops radiating an enthusiasm in which his workers could share. Now in the midst of overwhelming success, the greatly increased Ford work force had become isolated — and disenchanted, a situation certainly mirrored in most large industries across the country. One day as Henry toured a machine shop with his young son Edsel, they happened upon two men fighting. It embarrassed him. Why had it happened, why had there been that look of hatred in the men's faces upon the sight of him? What would it cost, Henry wondered to Jim Couzens, to make his men "glad to see us when we come along." His answer came the afternoon of January 5th. The Ford company, it was announced, was reducing the work day to eight hours (from the usual ten), converting the factory from two shifts to three and instituting a five-dollar basic wage (a raise doubling the standard going rate).

Alvan Macauley of Packard called Charles Sorensen in horror that same day, Hugh Chalmers pronounced the plan incredibly radical, *The New York Times* asked Henry point blank if he was a Socialist, and a mass meeting of Socialists said it was a "detestable trap." The *Wall Street Journal* was absolutely aghast.

Henry's answer was simple. "Well, you know," he told an associate, "when you pay men well you can talk to them." Publicly he announced that the $5 day was "a plain act of social justice," it was both "profit sharing and efficiency engineering." Henry was becoming ridiculously wealthy, his company's coffers had $28 million excess by the end of 1913, he had shared his success with the consumer by lowering the price of his product, it was time to share the largesse with his workers. Both would benefit. Years later it would be widely recognized that mass production could only exist by being fed with a constantly increasing purchasing power on the part of labor.

For a while it appeared that every worker in America wanted to work for Henry. They stormed his plant, blocked the streets, jammed the gates. Inside the plant some enthusiastic workers had to be slowed down because they got ahead of the assembly line. A thousand T's a day were built during February of 1914 and by June Ford workers were getting one out every half minute.

For a while it seemed, too, that there were as many rumors about the T's as there were the cars themselves. Henry would sell them for $100 each on his birthday or the day Virginia went dry; he would give them away to anyone sending in four dimes, the mint letters of which spelled F.O.R.D. All this was utter nonsense, of course, but the rumors were widely circulated and served to keep Henry's name in public view — understandably he rather enjoyed that. In the press, however, he was not generally viewed with quite the same affection as it was clear the mass of America felt for him. It is safe to say that Henry Ford might have been one rich man whose wealth was never envied or condemned in those salad days.

Henry Ford's concern for his workers was deeply felt, and the Sociological Department he had set up to administer the $5 plan, while it smacks of Big Brotherism today — as it did to some even then — was nonetheless an earnest attempt to insure that Ford workers might appropriately cope with their newfound affluence. Certainly with regard to the immigrant workers, the programs were immeasurably beneficial. And his policy with regard to the handicapped — thousands of those considered unemployable by industry at large worked for

Ford — was both beneficient and enlightened.

Not so enlightened was Henry's plan to stop the First World War. He was a pacificist, believing with disarming sincerity that war was immoral because it killed people while others made a profit. Rather naively he thought he could do something about it. In the fall of 1915 after reading that 20,000 soldiers had been killed in Europe on a single day, their deaths having had no effect whatsoever on the war's course, he proclaimed his willingness to spend half his fortune to shorten the carnage. (Henry had, so Mark Sullivan affectionately mused, "a good deal of practical faith in the power of half his fortune.") But the peace ship he sponsored and sent to Europe failed in its task — and his efforts were lampooned generally in the press ("It is not Mr. Ford's purpose to make peace; he will assemble it," said the Boston *Traveler*) and by government officials both in America and abroad (Queen Victoria's prime minister Asquith jocularly referred to the *Oscar II* as "a vessel propelled by a gentleman named Ford, said to be a manufacturer of perambulators.") Of the venture Henry regretted only its failure: "I wanted to see peace. I at least tried to bring it about. Most men did not even try."

Henry Ford's pacifist efforts had two results — in addition to further making news about their proponent and his company, and the still debatable effects they had on the peace movement in general. The first was immediate: Jim Couzens, who did not share Henry's views, resigned his position with the Ford company in 1915. The second was the libel action brought against the *Chicago Tribune* by Henry for that paper's having called him an anarchist. The suit was filed in 1916; it was delayed going to trial three years. Once in court, however, matters moved. The jury selection was swift, one juror confiding his ownership of a Model T but "That would not prejudice me against Mr. Ford." Henry's day in court, unfortunately, was not his best. Under defense questioning, he displayed rather vague notions about America's past and promulgated his famous "history is bunk" dictum (this from the man who would give America a remarkable museum and the gracious beauty of Greenfield Village which serves history as valuably today as any textbook); suggested that Benedict Arnold was a writer (he probably confused him with Horace L. Arnold who had written a Ford engineering manual); and refused to read any of the material the *Tribune* attorney pressed upon him ("I am not a fast reader. I have hay fever and I'd make a botch of it.") This last spread rumors that Henry Ford was an illiterate, rather vicious ones apparently, for a Ford biographer in the Twenties felt compelled to issue a forceful denial ("Mr. Benson saw him write many times") and deboss an example of Henry's penmanship on the cover of his book. Henry's exasperation during the proceedings was ill-concealed, though he was one up on his inquisitors during some exchanges. "What was the United States originally," the *Tribune* attorney leered. "Land, I guess," said Henry.

The *Tribune* trial didn't enhance Henry's reputation in learned circles, though doubtless many Americans sympathized with his uneasiness on the stand, probably not recalling themselves the reasons for the War of 1812. Ostensibly he won the case, but the victory was meaningless — and the whole sorry affair would have been better forgotten.

The *Tribune*'s questioning of Henry's patriotism was absurd, of course, for even before America's entrance in the war Ford was producing for it. For years after Henry displayed a framed letter from London relating how Model T's had saved British troops from starvation during a particularly difficult engagement. As a troop and supply carrier Henry's "Hunka Tin" — à la Kipling — was an in-

valuable Ally asset, and the Model T was even recommended for the Distinguished Service Cross for its efforts in the battle of the Argonne. Henry had meant his company's military participation — it was a vast one, ambulances, helmets, shells, armor plate, the Liberty engine, Eagle boats, tanks — to be strictly non-profit, this reflecting his views on war in general. He announced his intention in this regard early, but there were to be problems all along. Ford stockholders couldn't be expected to share Henry's views, and they didn't. He then agreed to return 58.5 percent (his percentage of Ford stock) of the profits to the government — and left it to Washington to figure out what that was. That took the government a good five years, which irked Henry mightily, so that by the time the figure was computed (March 1924) Henry had long since become bored with the matter. Henry's patience quotient diminished as year passed year. This combined with his own reckoning — a demonstrable one — that his company had not claimed reimbursement for expenditures or had absorbed losses well in excess of any profits made probably lay behind his disregarding the $926,780 "bill" the government finally sent him. The free publicity of handing over a check would have been worth at least the million dollars involved — which Henry could well afford. No, nonpayment was not a matter of poverty, it was instead a matter of principle — and if it demonstrated an inconsistency in Henry's character, it showed his flowering obstinance as well.

Henry's ideas regarding his conduct of the Ford Motor Company were equally resolute. Year by year the price of the Model T had been lowered, and in August of 1916 Henry ordered another price slashing: eighty dollars off the touring car ($440 to $360), with commensurate reductions for runabout ($390 to $345) and sedan ($640 to $545). A couple of weeks later he declared the cessation of special dividends to stockholders and the plowing back into the company of some $58 million of accumulated profits. He also had some rather tart things to say about stockholders being non-producers receiving unearned dividends from profits which belonged rightly to the workers and their work. This naturally pleased Ford shareholders not at all, and the Dodge brothers — prominent among that group — brought suit against Ford in late 1916 for, among other considerations, "reasonable dividends." Litigation dragged through three years — Henry lambasting the Dodges for the absurdity of challenging a policy that had escalated their $10,000 worth of stock into $50,000,000. In the end the courts declared the Dodges were entitled to their dividends — a landmark decision, by the way — which a miffed Henry had to promptly pay.

About a month and a half before the court decision (on December 30th, 1918) and perhaps in anticipation of it, Henry had taken step number one to insure that such challenges to the way he wished to run his company would never again arise. He resigned from Ford. His twenty-six-year-old son Edsel was named president — and the motoring world, its collective mouth agape, anxiously wondered what was next. Henry let the word out two months later; a new company, that was his plan, and a new car to compete with the Model T. To the cries of the Dodges that he couldn't do that, Henry said why not? Why not indeed! Ford Motor Company stock suddenly became a *very* salable commodity and the rumors regarding the company (adroitly fed to the press by Henry) frightened off potential bidders, save for a group of agents acting on behalf of a mysterious unidentified party. They eventually succeeded in buying out every minority stockholder. Only the last to give in — Couzens — was absolutely aware, before he decided to sell, of the man for whom the agents were working. When the last option was lined up, Henry Ford "danced a jig all around the room." Never before had one man con-

1920 Depot Wagon / Henry Ford Museum

1922 Speedster by Ames / Harrah's Automobile Collection

1924 Speedster by Mercury / Harrah's Automobile Collection

1923 Fronty Ford / Owner: Robert Burze

trolled completely an organization of this size. The Ford Motor Company was all Henry's now.

To gain this control Henry had secured a temporary bank loan of $75,000,000, the stockholders having been paid off handsomely at a rate of $12,500,000 for each $5000 they had invested, save for Couzens who received $13,000,000. Henry neither liked nor trusted bankers, and it was his intention to repay the loan promptly by the April 1921 due date — and get the financial community off his back for keeps. Unfortunately he hadn't reckoned with the postwar depression of 1920, which affected even Model T sales. But he soon solved that by the simple expedient of shipping thousands of unasked-for Model T's to surprised dealers, demanding from them payment in cash or the loss of their franchise. A few dealers took the latter course, but not many — most simply secured bank loans themselves, paid Ford, who in turn paid off his bank debt. Whatever one's thoughts on the Ford strategy, the plan succeeded beautifully and with the business upswing Ford dealers had little trouble unloading the C.O.D. T's.

What had made possible Henry's coup both in getting total control of his company and in sailing through the depression on the coattails of his dealers was, of course, the Model T. Henry, as an admiring biographer wrote, had thrown "his mind into 'high'," and his Model T powered him through. Model T Power! No more potent a force was there in the automobile world than the sturdy car that clattered the nation's highways in numbers not exceeded by the total output of all other American manufacturers combined.

By the early Twenties the Model T seemed unconquerable. She was the beloved Lizzie, the endearing flivver — the origins of both nicknames having since been obscured, if they ever were known. Some say Lizzie perhaps arose from "lizard," the Model T sharing the attributes of the hardy, fast little reptile, or perhaps from the frequent appearance of the name for one's favorite horse or aunt; flivver might have been derived from a "for the liver" joke about the T, one of the thousands which asked such questions as "what shock absorbers do you use on your Ford" — the answer to that one being "the passengers." Another gaining wide currency in the Teens was "what's the difference between a 1910 model Ford and a 1916?" The answer there was "six years." But Lizzie had fooled them for the 1917 model year with a new set of clothes. "Yes, it's a Ford," the New York *World* had captioned the picture of the new T, its radiator now a black steel shell, its hood streamlined out of its old angularity, its fenders curved and crowned, nickel taking the place of brass, an electric horn replacing the Klaxon. There had been — and would be — a number of engineering refinements, a less clattersome muffler, finer machining, the use of new, lighter and stronger metals in various engine parts. By 1920 even the electric starter was available on any Lizzie — as an option only. But early in the Twenties Henry said enough was enough — and began a steadfast resistance to any further tampering. It didn't seem to matter for a while. The Model T rolled on as ever.

It might have been, as Lee Strout White concluded, that a T owner never regarded his purchase as a complete, finished product: "When you bought a Ford, you figured you had a start — a vibrant, spirited framework to which could be screwed an almost limitless assortment of decorative and functional hardware." A $60,000,000 industry grew up supplying for the T what Henry wouldn't. He made a lot of men very rich. Remembered best today were those accessory manufacturers who offered, for a price, to make the T a sporting lady: Craig-Hunt, R. M. Roof (Laurel), Rajo, Morton & Brett. A Rajo 8-valve head helped a special T racer, Noel Bullock driving, to win Pikes Peak in 1922. And

1926 Runabout / Owner: William T. Tyrrel

1926 Touring Car

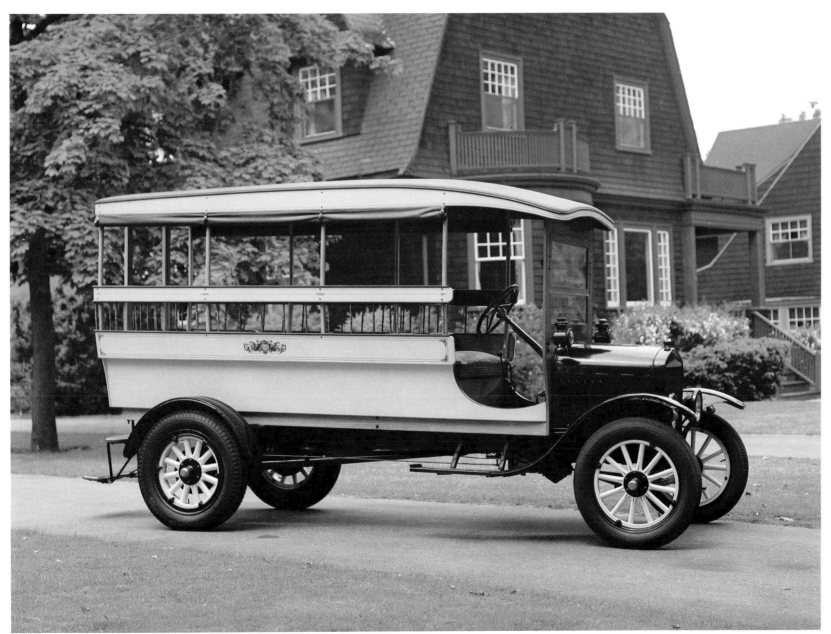

1926 Depot Wagon

1926 Tudor Sedan / Owner: R.E. Crane

the Chevrolet brothers tweaked the T into the fuming Fronty Fords that revolutionized dirt track racing and brought further renown to the company that by itself was legend.

Henry Ford probably paid but scant attention to the latter-day racing efforts inspired by his Model T. His increasing obstinance regarding the permanence of its design left him with free time to pursue other ventures. He bought a railroad, a saw mill, a glass works, sixteen coal mines and vast stretches of timber and agricultural land. He dug a canal, built a fleet of Great Lakes steamers — and some quite interesting airplanes. And there was the River Rouge plant and Muscle Shoals. Significantly, in the early Thirties, Henry was to lament to a *Fortune* writer, "The Rouge is so big that it is no fun anymore."

About 1922 there arose a Ford-for-President movement of some significance. *Collier's Weekly* gave Henry an eight-to-five lead over the incumbent Warren Harding. But Henry's good wife Clara, who had supported him wholeheartedly through the years, put her foot down now. Her husband wouldn't make a good President, she said, and if he "wants to go to Washington, he can go, but I'll go to England!" After the death of Harding in 1923, Henry announced that he intended to support the new President for reelection — and Calvin Coolidge thanked him. For years he carried a newspaper editorial in his wallet averring that the editors cared not who made the laws of the land so long as Ford made its flivvers. Henry's presidential interest had been half-hearted at best.

He was acquainted with and visited the Presidents whose reigns of power were abbreviated political variations of the not-to-be-denied power he had as head of Ford. But his closest friends were Thomas Alva Edison, naturalist John Burroughs and Harvey S. Firestone, with whom Henry enjoyed innumerable camping trips and upon whom Henry played many of the practical jokes which amused him so. It was said that Henry personally whittled the wooden croutons he put in Harvey Firestone's soup one day. Henry was a "lovable man," John Burroughs said; he was the camp cut-up according to Thomas Edison. The quartet was inseparable — until their excessive fame by the mid-Twenties turned their camping treks into mob scenes.

Years later it would become fashionable to decry Henry Ford's insensitivity to the graces of life. And it is true that his tastes were simple; grandeur wasn't his style. On visiting J. P. Morgan once, he remarked guilelessly, "It is very interesting to see how the rich live." Fair Lane, the fabulous house he built for Clara along the River Rouge (where they both had been born and grew up; where they were married) was a haven — a fortress almost — against the outside world, where Clara could pursue her gardening, delight in her music room, and in the evenings in the library read to her husband the novels of Thackeray and Wells' *Outline of History*. Though he had them by the score, Henry disliked servants; they might laugh at him, he thought, because he enjoyed eating potatoes with the skins on. He adored square dancing. Henry was against smoking and for Prohibition. His antipathies extended to the Ku Klux Klan, the Knights of Columbus and the Masons* (all of which "can be traced back to Wall Street," he said, that thoroughfare representing another pet Ford aversion.) The campaign he launched quite sincerely to "uplift" the Jews was a black mark against him — his worst — for which he ultimately apologized. Still it would require only the most unforgiving nature to attribute evil motivation to Henry's prejudices. Instead he reflected the traditions and values of the agrarian America from whence he came. It typifies to note that in 1923 Edgar A. Guest authored a piece for *American Magazine* entitled "Henry Ford Talks About His Mother." The sentimentality

that conjures is cloying today; at the time, it was but part and parcel of the folk legend that was Henry Ford.

Henry was very like his Model T—and both were fast becoming, as the French so subtly put it, of a certain age. In 1924 he was sixty-one; she, sixteen. On June 15th that year the 10,000,000th Tin Lizzie left the factory (there would be 5,000,000 more), its price in touring car form to be lowered to $290 (the all-time low) in December. That year the T outsold its nearest competitor six to one; the year following the ratio would be four to one, then almost two to one. Those were ominous forebodings, difficult to ignore. Only Henry continued to believe that his Tin Lizzie remained the American automotive dream. To him, getting from one place to another was all that should be expected of a car. But the rest of America expected more, and the Model T wasn't delivering it. Lizzie had never been a coquette, but she had possessed a certain appeal; now she was a creaky old lady and she wasn't desired very much anymore.

Henry did allow some modest concessions to the reality of it all. Between 1908 and 1911 the company had advertised extensively, but the $5 day, Henry's various news-getting forays and the omnipresent Ford jokes and songs led him to believe advertising was no longer necessary—it wasn't until the summer of 1923 that the company reestablished the advertising department that had ceased to function during the First World War. As for the product advertised, there were changes too, most significantly the reintroduction of colors other than black in 1926 when quick-drying lacquers became available, the option of wire wheels (balloon tires were introduced in 1925), a nickel-plated radiator shell and the removal of the fuel tank forward into the cowl. Body and frame had been lowered for a more streamlined appearance, though Will Rogers suggested it was "to lessen the distance of the fall." The humorist's conclusions regarding the "new" T: "Why, it almost seems like changing the Statue of Liberty's dress from a flowing robe to Plus Fours." In short, not a ringing endorsement.

In September of 1926 Cannon Ball Baker, who was willing to take anything on four wheels across the continent, left Perth Amboy, New Jersey, solo, with a T in high gear — and five days two hours thirteen minutes later arrived in Los Angeles. It was a record. Some sort of musical history was probably made, too, when in 1927 the Boston Symphony performed a fourteen-minute "joyous epic, fantasy for orchestra" composed by Harvard music professor T. S. Converse and entitled "Flivver Ten Million." Conductor Serge Koussevitzky had only reluctantly included the composer's honks, rattles, squeaks and crashes, all of which were favorably reviewed in the *Boston Transcript* and *New York Times*.

That was probably the way the Tin Lizzie would have wanted to go — in the familiar surroundings of cacophonous sound. Just a few weeks after Lizzie's concert debut, the last Model T officially left the Ford factory. It was May 27th.** Her passing was mourned by tens of thousands, from the octogenarian in California who had written Ford that he had gone West to die but began driving a Model T instead and his health improved — to Sinclair Lewis whose widow would later reminisce that not even the Nobel Prize had been as gratifying to her husband as the ownership of his first Model T. But none would mourn her passing as much as Henry.

---

*Interestingly, Henry himself later became a 33rd degree Mason. He remained, as always, a most contradictory gentleman.

**Serial number records end with this date, although production actually continued through June.

PART THREE:
Model A

As losing battles go, Henry Ford fought a splendid one. No doubt about that. On January 20th, 1926, Ernest Kanzler had submitted what in effect was his letter of resignation when he handed Henry a lengthy and well considered memo stating as delicately as possible that the Model T was ruining the company. Mr. Kanzler was a second vice-president of The Ford Motor Company and brother-in-law to Henry's son Edsel, but six months after the memo he was out of a job. Edsel, of course, was the Ford company president, as he had been since 1919 when Henry gave him the title during that bit of derring-do earlier noted which effectively eliminated the Dodge brothers and all other minority stockholders from Ford affairs. But unfortunately all Henry allowed Edsel was the title. A British correspondent probably said it best when, after a trip to this country and at a loss for words to describe the colossus he had seen that was the Ford empire, marvelled instead that "over the whole concern, and every part of its organization down to the smallest detail, Henry Ford, a thin, elderly, white haired and altogether efficient man, holds absolute and despotic sway."

But the Ford Motor Company was headed for trouble—everybody within the firm knew that, except Henry. And from without, the word in the industry was that Henry Ford was losing his grip, the "vast virgin field" he developed with his Model T was being defiled by sprightlier, more appealing and only slightly more expensive cars. Installment buying—which Henry disliked intensely—was bringing these cars within the reach of the average Model-T-type buyer, and others of that genre were finding the new but burgeoning used car market a worthy avenue to travel to acquire a considerably more expensive, glamorous and commodious car at Model T prices, or below. True, Ford was still building vastly more cars than *anybody* else, but *everybody* else was now building more cars than Ford. In 1924, 700,000 more Model T's had been built than all other makes combined, in 1925 350,000 less—and in 1926 when, significantly, the company began suppressing the figures, Model T production accounted for but a third of the industry total. The writing was on the wall. Henry Ford just didn't want to read it.

It was during 1926 too that a survey of the University of Michigan's School of Business Administration discussed what planned obsolescence—for good or ill, it was here to stay—meant to the industry, and the Model T for that year had given a cursory nod to what would soon become known as the annual facelift. But it was not enough; neither were the reductions in price, two of them that year—in February and June. Anent the latter *The New York Times* carried follow-up stories about the stir of interest and the "keen competition foreseen" in the wake of the Ford announcement, but *Automotive Industries* was perhaps nearer the truth in remarking that "a Ford price cut . . . no longer commands the attention that it once did." Economy alone, it appeared, just wouldn't sell cars anymore.

Henry Ford continued to insist that his car's only problem was the pleasant one of not being able to make enough of them. If sales fell off—as they did—it was the fault of the dealers, not the T. And Edsel watched the ranks of Ford agents dwindle month by month, with defections to Chevrolet, Star, Whippet and others, such turnovers in the twenty-one months leading to October of 1926 ranging as high as a frightening forty-five percent in Salt Lake City. As early as June newspapers carried reports that a new Ford was in the offing—they were immediately denied. So were all the others that followed.

"Ford To Fight It Out With His Old Car" was the way *The New York Times*

HOW DO YOU FOLLOW A LEGEND? WITH ANOTHER ONE,

put it in the eight-column banner headline for its Sunday automotive section of December 26th, 1926. The accompanying story was almost wistful; as reporter James C. Young wrote, "In these quiet days of the Christmas season the gray wizard of Dearborn walks through the interminable miles of his plants with much to ponder. Many departments of those plants are deserted now, and his footfall sounds loudly in the unaccustomed stillness. All around him are the evidences of his power, of the truly stupendous industry built from an idea. For the first time in the annals of that industry Ford domination has been seriously challenged. Its creator sees lesser rivals growing great and beginners in the trade commanding a sizable share of the whole. Not only has the challenge been given, but boldly pressed. The year coming to an end was marked by a concentrated attack upon Ford supremacy such as it never withstood before. Another and stronger attack lies ahead, launched from every side and all sides at once."

Henry Ford appeared unmoved. The Model T would remain, any experimental projects in work had one important purpose: "They keep our engineers busy—prevent them tinkering too much with the Ford car." Still, everyone wondered. In February the following year, *The American Review of Reviews* published an article titled "What Is Henry Ford Going To Do?" Since it was written by Samuel Crowther, who was pretty much Henry's Boswell, it had a ring of authority. No changes would be made that could not be incorporated in the existing car, and the crisis in the low-priced market was one "in which the Ford Company is the least involved."

Moody's Investment Service was equally sanguine; Ford could come back at any time, it was not low-priced car competition that was hurting the company,

OF COURSE

but inroads from the medium-priced range. Yet, when the *Detroit News* reported an off-the-cuff—and alleged—remark by Henry that he would be building a new medium-priced car, everyone scoffed. As *Automobile Topics* noted, Henry Ford's enthusiasm for the middle ground in the industry had ever been restrained, "and with Ford a restrained enthusiasm is about as animated and informing as a Coolidge breakfast."

It was the low-priced field that had to be the concern, Chevrolet specifically. In January 1927 some 73,676 of the new model Chevies rolled out of the factory, nearly—and incredibly—30,000 more than January of '26. "Here is a car that in the past has been thought of conventionally as the sliding-gear competitor of the Ford, as a car built strictly to price standards," the press said. "But lo! in its 1927 dress it makes a very definite style appeal." With Chevrolet leading the way, General Motors had had its greatest year ever—"by a ridiculously large margin"—in 1926. Nineteen twenty-seven promised to be even greater.

The industry was agog. "Politeness and the ethics of business," John C. Wetmore wrote in *Motor West*, prevented manufacturers from discussing the Ford dilemma but there was no denying their plans were based "to some considerable extent, to put it mildly, on expectations of a continuation of the Ford sales retrogression for some time or at least until the persistently rumored and the still even more persistently doubted new Ford models make their appearance." As Norman G. Shidle commented in *Automotive Industries*, "By talking to any ten men in the [trade] it is easy to learn 5000 things that Ford is going to do and an equal number that people think he ought to do. . . ." Most of the talk remained centered on a new model—in February, more rumors; in March, a bold prediction in the *Daily Metal Trade*; in April, still more rumors, May the same. On May 18th Ford spokesman W. J. Cameron denied reports of a new car—insofar as he knew. Someone hadn't told him, because one week later the Ford Motor Company announced that a vehicle to replace the Model T would be forthcoming.

Henry Ford was less than happy, though the press at the time couldn't know that. The months preceding had been stormy ones at Ford Motor Company, Ernest Kanzler's leave-taking being followed by numerous others among the executive staff, but even so those remaining had grown steadily more vociferous in their assessment of the Model T situation. Edsel had become more and more assertive—so much so that the working relationship between father and son often had to be strained through intermediaries carrying messages between their respective offices. In one fit of pique Henry asked Charles Sorensen to order his son "to clear out, go to California, and stay there until ordered to come back." Sorensen didn't do it—and Henry eventually cooled down. Eventually, too, it was probably Edsel who persuaded Henry of the crying need for a car other than the T—and right away.

The elder Ford's reluctance to replace the Model T, it should be noted, was not solely sentimental. What he desired was simply that the car to follow it be as startling in its day as the T had been in its, and Henry just hadn't come up with one yet. He had an idea, one to which engineer Eugene J. Farkas had been lending his talents since 1924: the eight-cylinder X engine, four pairs of cylinders on a central crank, four cylinders up, four down, in the form of the letter "X." But this radical design—Henry's pet project—was still in developmental throes, slowed possibly by the six-cylinder engine experiments requested by Edsel Ford and

Kanzler, when Henry was forced to concede the end of the Model T. In eulogy to Tin Lizzie, the Ford company paraded an overwhelming series of statistics to witness the revolution that the T had wrought, concluding that "before the last of the Model T Ford cars shall have gone to the junk-heap, the entire fleet of 15,-000,000 will have . . . traveled more than 1,185,000,000,000 miles." Allowing for the happy error regarding the ultimate destination of all Model T's, the statement spoke volumes about what the T had accomplished. "Pretty good for one small car," Henry Ford remarked wistfully. Small wonder that its creator wished its successor to be as revolutionary, that he hoped the X would follow the T.

But it was not to be. There simply wasn't time. The exact chronology here is a bit fuzzy, but it appears that in the midst of denials from Ford there had been some work done on the T's successor during 1926, an oral order from Henry to proceed with a design for a four-cylinder car coming perhaps as early as August. Why a four? Henry wouldn't consider a six—there was "no excuse" for a six-cylinder car, he contended; it had all the engineering difficulties of an eight and none of its advantages—and besides if Ford built one he would be following, not leading, the industry. And the X-eight? Well, that experimental job had to be dropped when engineer Farkas advised that success was years away. The new car would be called the Model A, so designated to allay any suspicions it might be thought a revamped Model T.

First blueprints of the four—very sketchy ones—were ready mid-January 1927, and work proceeded at a pace that can only be called phenomenal. Of that Henry Ford later said only: "Edsel and I decided on the wheelbase and size right away. . . . After that it was a matter of working things out on the drawing board until we got them right." Among the engineers assigned to the project were Eugene Farkas of X engine development, Joseph Galamb who had worked so skillfully on the T, Frank Johnson from Lincoln, and a newcomer named Laurence S. Sheldrick. Pete Martin and Charles Sorensen offered advice, Edsel brought his heightened sense of aesthetics to the body design—and of course there was Henry.

Initial reluctance aside, once the project was under way, Henry Ford devoted all his energies to it. "Sixty-four today and the biggest job of my life ahead," he would tell *The New York Times* on his birthday in July, beginning that day by rising at seven, meeting the leader of his orchestra at seven thirty to select the music for the country club dance, and arriving at the factory at eight as usual to meet with his engineers and orchestrate the Model A. He had even foregone his annual vacation camping trip with Thomas Edison and Harvey Firestone.

There were problems of course. Henry's tardiness in preparing a replacement for the T would have been sufficient cause for consternation. But this combined with the Ford idea that research was most happily defined by rule of thumb. Expansive scientific facilities, centralized engineering laboratories, proving grounds—none of these did the Ford Motor Company have, nor did Henry Ford consider them necessary. His approach was the pragmatic, not the esoteric—if a new type of axle was needed, it should be developed where the axles were made; research should be diffused, with "suggestions and aid in the solution of problems [coming] from either chief executives or men in the shops," the resulting competition would be healthy. Cars should be tested on the sort of roads on which they would be used (the Dearborn police took a dim view of this)—and reports back from official tester Ray Dahlinger were right to the point; the car was either

1928 Model 60-A Fordor Sedan / Owner: Norman Orton

1928 Model 35-A Standard Phaeton / Henry Ford Museum

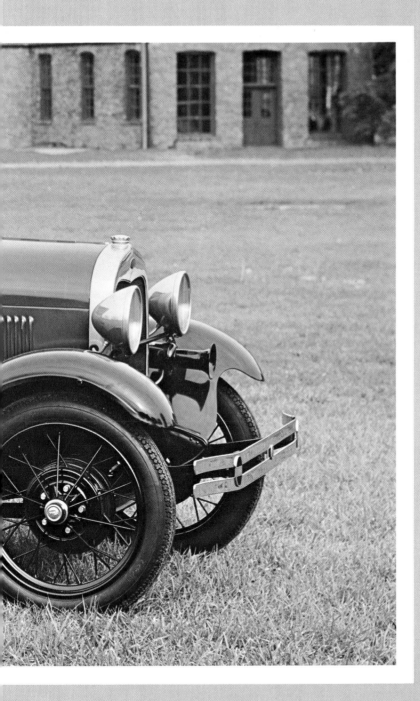

"damn good" or "no damn good." Although in retrospect such methods might be loudly decried as slapdash, retrospect must also recognize that these same methods produced the Model T. And, following it, the A. And make no mistake about it, the Ford Model A was a fabulous car. Just ask any automotive enthusiast who owns one.

If there be one reason that could be pointed to for the preeminent worthiness of the Model A, it was simply that Henry Ford built it. Integrity of product was his paramount consideration in the building of an automobile; as historians Allan Nevins and Frank Ernest Hill elaborated, "consumer demand came second, and any thought of profits was incidental." True, certainly; Henry never really lost the almost endearing arrogance that led him to assume the public would gratefully accept whatever he offered them—and factors of economy were seldom considered by him, witness his determination to use costly steel forgings in the Model A rather than less expensive stampings and malleable castings. Henry in fact had only the most ephemeral notions of what the Model A cost him. When asked later about it, he casually subtracted the amount of money he had in the bank when the Model A was finished from the figure when it was begun and came up with $100,-000,000. In truth, with retooling, loss of profits during the changeover, et al., the actual figure was nearer $250,000,000. Henry Ford wouldn't have blinked at that either.

And he kept his eyes wide open throughout the Model A development. Its engine would follow the Model T only generally in being an L-head four-cylinder unit, with such welcome improvements over the T as a water pump (replacing the T's thermosyphon) and battery distribution ignition (replacing the previous magneto and vibrator coil). Bore-stroke dimensions of 3⅞ by 4¼ were suggested by Sheldrick and agreed to by Ford, Sorensen and Martin. This worked out to 200.5 cubic inches, the T had been 176.7. Henry wanted at least forty horsepower (for a road speed of between 50 and 60 mph) at no more than 2200 rpm (this to keep engine vibration at a minimum, fuel economy at a maximum and assure a long operating life.) T'was easier said than done. The first try worked its way up to twenty-two horsepower, only two more than the T. Harold Hicks, Ford's chief aircraft engineer was called in, whipped out his slide rule, calculated a while and said, sure, he thought he could do it. It was April 1927. He asked for two months, was given one. Three weeks later he had the engine up to forty, with a redesign of the manifold for better breathing, an opening of the water passage around the exhaust valve, and the replacement of the Holley carburetor by a Zenith. This last, it was feared, Henry would never go for, he being a bosom friend of George Holley's, but Henry did—and in typical form. He looked at the Zenith carburetor and said, okay, but there were too many bolts holding it together. Hicks told Zenith, Zenith reduced the number from fourteen to two. Henry looked at it again. Still too many, he said. The Model A carburetor was introduced with but a single bolt.

Simplicity was sought throughout. Henry liked his idea of a single control for choking and adjusting the carburetor from the dash panel—no other car had it; it was incorporated. Difficulty of manufacture bothered him not; he insisted on an expensive "mushroom" foot for the engine valve stems, thus giving the Ford valves a longevity equal to the rest of the engine, without adjustment.

Edsel Ford had by now become a more dominant force in company affairs, and Henry had to admit—and he did, with pride—that "we've got a pretty good man

1928 Model 49-A Special Coupe / Owner: Walt Bendel

1928 Model 82-A Closed Cab Pick-Up / Owner: Glenn Johnson

1928 Model AR Tudor Sedan / Owner: Richard Fischbach

in my son. He knows style—how a car ought to look. And he has mechanical horse sense, too." Harold Hicks agreed, commenting with regard to Edsel's contribution to the Model A engine that he "knew the right way to get power out of a job was to get the stuff in there and explode it." Still, relations between father and son had become sticky again when talk got around to the Model A's transmission. Henry's beloved planetary would have to go, Edsel insisted, and though his father mused about an automatic planetary transmission, its development would take years, Sorensen said, and now months, weeks, even days were precious. Henry Ford thought a sliding gear transmission lacked durability (forgetting conveniently that it stood up very well in the Lincoln motorcar, which he also happened to be building) and, most important, that it would be imitative. That in a Ford car Henry couldn't abide. Yet, with time against him, he had to compromise: The Model A would have a three-speed sliding gear transmission, a miniaturized version of the Lincoln's, designed by Frank Johnson. Henry Ford never really accepted it.

Compromising wasn't in Henry Ford's nature, but he was doing as much of that as dictating in the Model A. And he was approving a lot too. The cowl-mounted gravity fuel tank, for example, wasn't his idea, but he liked it, because it was extremely simple, it wasn't a vacuum tank system nor a fuel pump, both of which he abhorred and neither of which he would have permitted on his car. Then Edsel took the fuel tank and designed it right into the body cowl, a very interesting and unique styling idea. It was Edsel, too, who had insisted, from the beginning, on bringing the chassis lower to the ground than the T.

Overall chassis length (113 7/16 inches) and wheelbase (103½ inches) had been the earliest and most quickly arrived-at decisions approved by father and son for the Model A. Most everything else was a bit of a hassle. The Model A would have four wheel brakes, for instance, but not like any of the designs in vogue; Henry insisted on that. The knotty problem of doing it, devising a system that would not be complicated either in design or by possible patent infringement, was handed to Eugene Farkas. Cam-operated, wedge-adjusted brake shoes linked directly to the foot pedal bar was the result; Henry opted for an equalizer bar in the linkage, which Farkas and Sheldrick insisted would result in skids. It was tried, it did, and the solid cross-shaft system was returned. Improving the T's suspension was also Farkas' assignment, and he complied, with the proviso that Henry's two transverse spring system developed for the T be retained. The more conventional four lateral spring suspension was generally believed to be superior, but Henry was certain that was a fallacy, his system "being mechanically correct." With transverse suspension, the springs carried their own weight, relieving the axles of unsprung weight and allowing the use of lighter axles and bearings—lightness with strength, a Ford credo. Not until after Henry's death was any Ford built with lateral springs.

One day Henry Ford decided the Model A suspension was lacking something. He took a test car out for a drive—"Somebody must represent the public," he said—and charged it across an open field, arriving back from the bumpy trek with the order: "Rides too hard. Put on hydraulic shock absorbers." And so they were, the same Houdaille double-acting shocks being used on the high-priced Lincoln. "It was unheard of," Sheldrick said, for a car of its price class. The other manufacturers would have to follow a few years later. Henry Ford liked that.

On another day, in late July, Harold Hicks had a test car on the road—racing everything in sight, on Henry's orders—when another car swerved in front of him. In the crash Hicks and his mechanic were thrown through the windshield, both badly cut. Henry Ford and Edsel decided then and there that the A would have a windshield with laminated "safety glass." It was a first for a car in its price class too.

Actually the cross springs were about the only vestige of the T remaining in the A. The new car was mechanically up-to-date and thoroughly refined, "the cleaning up of the space under the hood" being among the improvements *Automotive Industries* would later comment favorably upon. Of course, under the T's hood one might have found baling twine, a coat hanger, paper clips, amid the maze of wires—the do-it-yourselfer would find less necessary to do in the A. And the accessory companies would feel a twinge in their financial coffers with the entrance of the liberally equipped A and the exit of the utilitarian T which had made so many of their fortunes. Even the Ford company would consider it provident to take a sideswipe at the old model by commenting in the A's brochure that "every precaution was taken to prevent squeaks, rattles and drumming sounds" in the body. Moreover, the A was attractive—a word unspoken in the T's presence—and would be made available its first year in nine body styles (phaeton, roadster, four coupes, two sedans and pickup truck) in a choice of four colors (with more variety to be had later with the addition of a number of new body styles built by Briggs and Murray) and at prices in the Model T range.

But what tickled Henry Ford most about it, according to associates' accounts of those final days of its birth, was its performance, Henry delighting in passing out orders to his fellows to "go out and drive a Model A wide open." Sixty-five miles an hour was a breeze, with five to twenty-five acceleration in eight and a half seconds—cars with two or four more cylinders had trouble equalling that. "Up to thirty miles an hour the model could skin the pants off anything on the road," beamed Harold Hicks.

And it could do it seemingly forever. The Model A's reliability is the stuff of which sonnets should be written. And its durability is legend. Utterly impervious it was to heat or cold—and apparently, too, to wear. Why? Perhaps because it was in ways overengineered. Many of its parts were strong enough to later be used in cars of twice the weight and three times the horsepower. The Model A was perhaps better than even its creators realized.

And what boggles the imagination is that it was all done so quickly and amidst the helter skelter of Henry Ford's *modus operandi*. Regarding the latter a writer of the period, Waldemar Kaempffert, noted: "As parts of the new car were fashioned, they were turned over to the testing staff with hardly a word. The testers proceeded to crush, twist, bend, and pound. They sent back transmission gears out of which they had succeeded in tearing teeth, and rear axles which they had reduced to junk. No suggestion of a possible method of making a part stronger or shaping it more nicely to suit its purpose—nothing but the battered part and the baldest statement of what happened in the testing machine. The designers made their own deductions and began anew. Thus engines, transmissions, axles, steering gears were tossed back and forth."

And as for the speed in which the A was created, one need only note that some parts went directly from drawing board into production, and as historian Leslie R. Henry has related, "in the latter stages of its birth, some of the plant layout and some of the new special machine tools were designed simultaneously with the

1929 Model 135-A Taxi-Cab / Owner: John Greenland

1929 Model 76-A Open Cab Pick-Up / Owner: Merle Smith

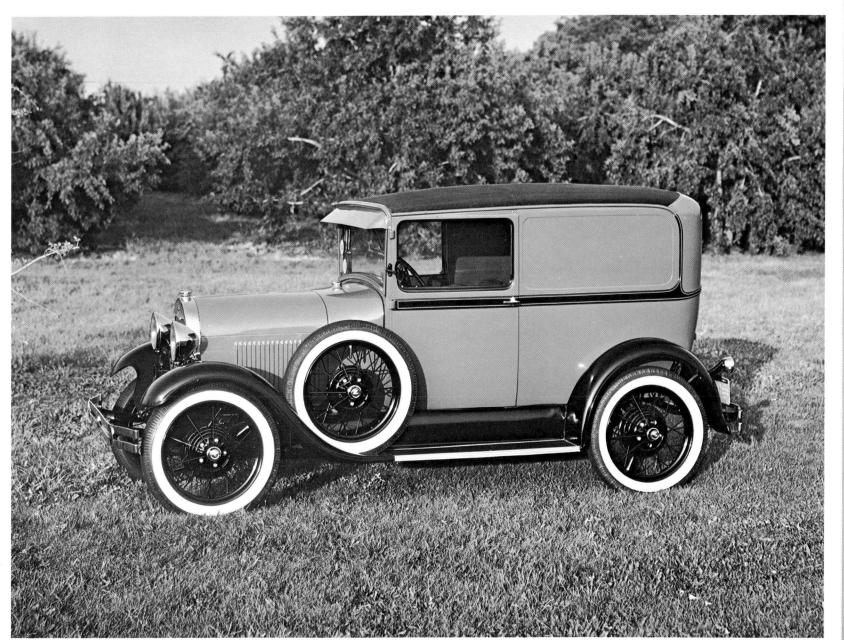

1929 Model 130-A De Luxe Delivery Van / Owner: James Hull

1929 Model 50-A Sport Coupe / Owner: Dan Gale

1929 Model 40-A Standard Roadster / Owner: John Morgan

1929 Model 60-B Fordor Sedan, with original showroom accessories / Owner: Ruben L. N

specific parts of the car each was to accommodate." Amazing, absolutely amazing.

Let's backtrack a bit now, and consider the Model A story from the point of view of the world outside the Ford company. Nothing that has been said so far was known.

On August 10th, 1927, Edsel Ford made the official announcement. "The new Ford automobile is an accomplished fact. The engineering problems affecting its design and equipment and affecting also its manufacture have all been solved. . . . The tests already made show it is faster, smoother, more rugged and more flexible than we had hoped for in the early stages of designing." He mentioned the new car's speed. And very little else.

It was page one news, the first word from Ford that the successor to the world's most famous car had become reality. The weeks from the May 25th announcement that the T would be replaced and the months of speculation before that had seen an absolutely unparalleled deluge of press reports about the new car, none emanating from the Ford Motor Company. The official Ford secrecy was tantalizing. Rumor ran rampant—and amok. The new car would be a Lincoln-Ford hybrid called the Linford, it would be named after Henry Ford's good friend Thomas Edison; it would have four cylinders, six cylinders, twelve cylinders; it would be available in three models, a four, six and an eight; it would be a solar-energized electric, a pocket diesel; it would have a four-speed hybrid transmission (two-speed planetary in conjunction with a two-speed gear on the rear axle). Cartoonists had a field day, one depicting the new model as a collapsible car which could be disguised as a trash can and parked on the sidewalk.

It was a rare day in 1927 when some reporter somewhere didn't divulge some new news about the T's successor. Seldom was the threshold of accuracy crossed. Save perhaps for reports like the one in the June 3rd, 1927 issue of the British *Autocar*—England was as agog as America—in which the editors put tongue firmly in cheek and announced: "The new model will . . . be more expensive to manufacture, economical in cost of operation, and superior in design and performance, and the specification may be stated with confidence to read as follows: — h.p., — cylinders, — x — mm. (—cc.), — clutch, — speed gear box, — transmission, — final drive, — springs, — tyres on — wheels, — wheel brakes, price £ —. Although more than one colour scheme is likely to be available, it is understood that the makers recommend some shade of black."

On June 22nd a perpetrator whose name history has never alleged swiped a series of ads from Ford's advertising agency in New York and handed them over to the New York News Bureau, which in turn released a story describing the new car. The ads were "preliminary and experimental," the specs "fictitious and imaginative" cabled the agency to every newspaper in the United States and Canada. Most killed the story, more than a few believing the entire episode was a clever Ford ploy for publicity. It wasn't; neither was the car depicted in the ads the Model A, it wasn't even ready by that date. Still if newspapers didn't carry the story, they carried the story of the story.

Believing one picture would be worth a thousand ill-founded words, legions of press photographers had descended upon Dearborn, abetted by hordes of amateurs, all anxious to come up with a photograph as coveted then as a picture of Greta Garbo is today. Whatever came out of the factory gates was snapped, and the blurred results found quick sale. (Of the total published, only two—one in

1929 Model 68-A Convertible Cabriolet / Owner: Carroll Vaughan

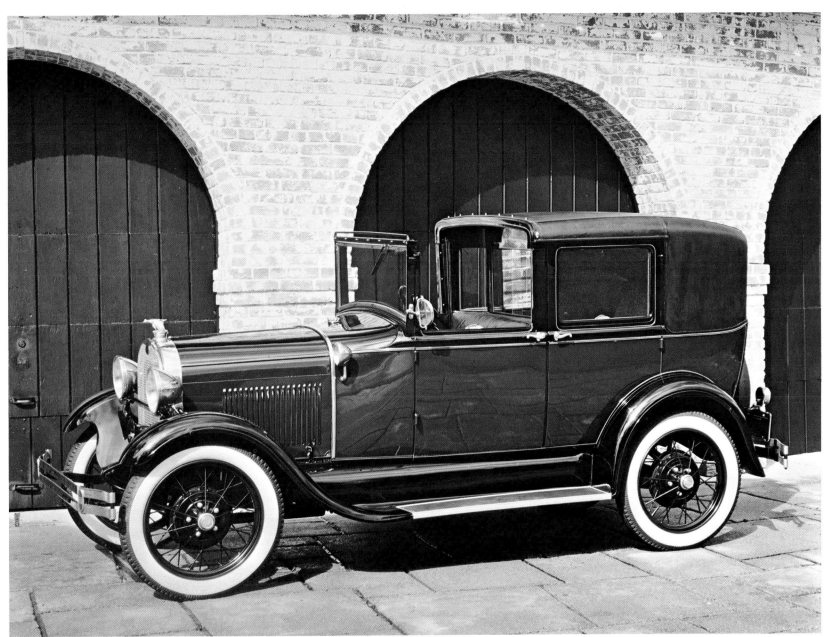

1929 Model 140-A Town Car / Owner: Owen Owens

the *Automotive Daily News,* another in the *Brighton* (Michigan) *Argus*—were really the Model A.)

Select dealers who had been given a sneak preview, Dearborn residents convinced they had seen it on the street, variously said the new model looked like a small Marmon . . . a miniature Lincoln . . . a diminutive LaSalle. All such conclusions were immediately rushed into print.

The suspense was incredible. Henry Ford was getting the sort of publicity even his money couldn't buy. He must have loved it.

Absolutes are a precarious business. But few bald statements can be projected with more assurance than the simple declaration that no car in history was more anxiously anticipated than the Model A Ford—or ever will be.

On October 11th Ford made its first public announcement in two months, the assembly line, Edsel said, would be rolling in a few days; on November 25th the company announced December 2nd as the date for the first public exhibition of the car. Show cars had been shipped to their various destinations completely shrouded, and under heavy guard, lest someone try to lift the veil of secrecy; those destined for England were sent "boxed up as luggage," also under guard. On the 26th was released a month-and-a-half-old teaser of a photo showing Henry Ford stamping "A1" on the engine block of the first Model A to leave the assembly line. (Only Henry and part of the engine could be seen.) On November 28th the Ford Motor Company began to advertise.

The new Ford advertising agency was N. W. Ayer & Son, having been selected in June and shortly thereafter contracting for huge amounts of newspaper space (five consecutive days of full-page advertisements in every one of America's two-thousand English-language dailies, total cost $1,300,000) without divulging the client's name. This was disclosed to the papers in the latter part of November, followed by sealed packages of plates with instructions they not be opened prior to publication. (In no case was the request ignored.)

The first ad—November 28th—was a masterpiece of the unspecific, a rambling announcement of the fact of the car, signed by Henry Ford and illustrated by his portrait. Mechanical specs were tossed out in ads two and three. Yet to come was a photograph, a quote of prices. But Wall Street was already reacting: "Announcement of New Car Sends Motors Down and Brings Rise in Accessories and Steel" ran one headline. It would be called a "Henry Ford market." On December 1st came the ad with photographs and prices. That day, too, had seen a special private showing at the Waldorf-Astoria for the elite of New York society (the press preview in Dearborn had been the day previous), and it was reliably reported that not once was the word "flivver" heard: "It was a new sensation for the Ford salesmen and executives who stood about in evening clothes, as if at a coming-out party, and they beamed all evening." Racing veteran George Robertson purred, "We don't brag about it, but it has done seventy-one miles an hour." Young ladies in sables said ". . . oooh."

On December 2nd—the day of the nationwide public showing—the last ad came, a wrap-up essentially of the previous four. The next day there were page one headlines in every city paper in the country. The Model A Ford had arrived!

For lack of a better cliché it might be said that all hell had broken loose. As the New York *World* remarked, "Excitement could hardly have been greater had Pah-wah, the sacred white elephant of Burma, elected to sit for seven days on the flagpole of the Woolworth Building." Nearly ten percent of the nation's pop-ulation—10,534,992 people—viewed the new Ford that first day. In New York crowds had begun lining up at three in the morning at the 1710 Broadway showroom of the company, a full six hours before the soaped windows were cleaned and the doors opened. Seventy-five policemen handled the crowds at Detroit's Convention Hall; a downpour in Charlotte, North Carolina, snow in Fargo, South Dakota and sub-zero temperatures in St. Paul, Minnesota couldn't keep the people away; a hastily constructed fence was necessary in Milwaukee "to prevent the packed masses of humanity from breaking the showroom windows." Dallas called it the "greatest [event] since the signing of the Armistice." Denver said it produced the most excitement in their city "since the robbery of the United States Mint."

It was exactly the sort of frenzied madness one associates with the Twenties. In New York when the sales literature ran out, Ford officials did likewise, to newsstands to purchase thousands of newspapers with the full-page ad. In other cities extra editions were profitably hawked, every Horatio Alger of a newsboy shouting the big news. Detectives prowled showrooms on the lookout in the morning for pickpockets, by the afternoon also for crafty swindlers who filched Ford sales pads and blithely began taking orders—and twenty-five dollar deposits.

The pandemonium didn't really let up for a week, by which time 25,000,000 people in the United States had filed into Model A showrooms or shows for a look at the new car. Add to that probably another million-and-a-half people who viewed the car overseas: from London, where an admission fee of 1 shilling and 6 pence (about thirty-six cents) was charged to view what the English called the "Reformed Lizzie," to Dublin, Paris, Berlin, Madrid, Antwerp, Brussels, Stockholm, Glasgow, Rotterdam, Zurich, Helsingfors (Helsinki), Athens, Cairo, Milan, Trieste, Tokyo, Osaka, Santiago, Rio de Janeiro, Montevideo, São Paulo, Pernambuco. In Havana extra mounted police were called in to handle the crowds, in Mexico City the police simply gave up and closed the showing early. In Lima the doors of the exhibition building were torn down.

With the hindsight of a week or so, the press began analyzing just what had happened. That it was the greatest publicity coup of modern times (perhaps all time) was the general consensus. As one writer observed, "Had the high talents of the late P.T. Barnum, the Brothers Ringling and Tex Rickard been united in one grand effort it is doubtful whether they could have brought to pass any such spectacle . . ." *The New Republic* looked at the matter intellectually: "Few news stories of recent years received more space. . . . None betokened more genuine and sustained interest. . . . Certainly no political, or international, or social, or artistic, or scientific news could approach it in popular validity."

With all the drama surrounding the introduction of the Model A, it might follow that the car itself would be anti-climactic. And in a way it was. Edsel Ford himself said there was nothing "radical" about the new car, that in fact it was more "conventional than old Model T," this alluding to its transmission and battery ignition design. But then the Model A had very little in common with the T—and this perhaps was revolution enough. Generally it was reviewed most enthusiastically in the press, though there were more than a few lamentations for the demise of the T. As a writer for the New York *Evening Post* mourned: "The old, black, rusty, cantankerous, obstinate, sputtering Ford brought wisdom to many and made many wise men go raving, tearing mad. This new lily-of-the-

1930 Model 68-B Convertible Cabriolet / Owner: John Tyrrell

82

1930 Model 35-B Standard Phaeton / Owner: Joel B. Feldman

1931 Model 45-B De Luxe Coupe / Owner: Walter H. Updike

1930 Model 40-B De Luxe Roadster / Owner: Herman Godwin

valley isn't going to teach us anything. It looks as if it would run indefinitely without complaint, which is all wrong. It is made for serenity and comfort which is all wrong. Where is the gas tank? Out front where it can be reached. Where is the timer? Up on top where it can no longer bark your knuckles. Where are the brake bands? In a ridiculously exposed position where their value as trainers of character and refined language is completely lost." Arguing that America was now entering an era of degenerate Roman luxury, he begged a return "to the pioneer days when we threw sand under the fan belt and tightened the horn with a dime."

Alas, those days were gone forever. The Model A was very much a car of its time and was applauded as such, worldwide. Though some on the Continent might cavil that its engine was, after all, typically American and not the small, high efficiency unit that had become the norm in overseas light car design, most echoed *The Autocar*'s view that "all models possess good lines and are distinctly of European appearance," which, to the foreign press, was fulsome praise indeed. And the prices, ranging from $385 to $570, were seen as genuine reductions over the Model T. The Tudor sedan, for example, at $495 was exactly the same in price; the Fordor sedan at $570 was but thirty dollars more; in all cases the refinements and improvements of the A over the T were the telling factors. The A was even more of a bargain than the T. And it was priced at least a hundred dollars less than the competition.

As for the competition, Henry Ford couldn't have been less concerned. During the T's waning days when its percentage of the market was slipping to a mere third, he had told Charles Sorensen not to worry, that twenty-five percent would satisfy him, and on his sixty-fourth birthday he advised a reporter: "We have no desire to take business away from any automobile manufacturer. . . . If any particular automobile company's success meant putting out of business some other automobile manufacturer, there would be no gain. It would only mean putting thousands of men out of work, letting valuable power go to waste and, maybe, throwing a great industry out of balance." His sincerity can't be doubted—as one of the richest men in the world, of course, Henry Ford could afford to be magnanimous. But his competition was . . . well, a bit more competitive.

On September 19th, 1927, *The New York Times* had editorialized that what the "public likes best is a slugging match" and one surpassing even a presidential campaign was upcoming: "the fight for the heavyweight national automobile championship between Henry Ford and General Motors." With the introduction of the A, General Motors president Alfred P. Sloan, Jr. took great pains to deny that any trade war with Ford was contemplated, though it was understood by everyone in the know that a new Chevrolet was waiting in the wings, and on January 11th Chevrolet sales vice-president R. H. Grant offered a cheering throng of his dealers in New York's Hotel Commodore "the challenging prediction" that Chevy would outsell the new Ford. The following day at the Roosevelt Hotel William C. Durant—not to be outdone—suggested his Star Four could do the same thing, which brought Durant dealers raucously to their feet.

A cynic once said that there are three kinds of lies: lies, damn lies and statistics. It would appear Ford's competitors longed for the truth of that, because the statistics were revealing. According to United States Department of Commerce figures, in 1927 nearly one million fewer cars were sold than in 1926, that figure neatly coinciding with the drop in Ford production concomitant with the discon-

1930 Model 82-B Closed Cab Pick-Up / Owner: Carroll Vaughan

1930 Model 45-B De Luxe Coupe / Owner: F. Doner

1930 Model 40-B De Luxe Roadster / Owner: J.R. Miller

tinuation of the Model T. And the National Automobile Chamber of Commerce, of which the Ford Motor Company was not a member, reported an increase in production of its member companies in the 175,000 unit range, a figure significantly low in light of the Ford shutdown. It would scarcely be a "damn lie" to infer then that a lot of people had waited for the new Ford.

Now the question was, when would they get one? While Henry Ford was vigorously denying the most ludicrous of rumors about the new car—that, for example, it would sell for a hundred dollars down and twelve fifty a month, with the company replacing it with a new one annually—his organization had been putting itself to the herculean task of retooling the Rouge plant (where the assembly line was moved in September of 1927) for mass production. Practically all the 5580 parts of the Model A were new, and this meant starting practically from scratch. It was, as reported in the press, "probably the biggest replacement of plant in the history of American industry." And somehow it was accomplished. On December 3rd, 1927, with son Edsel and grandsons Henry II and Benson at Detroit's Convention Hall, Henry Ford was telling reporters that production was now up to a hundred cars a day, with luck it would be up to a thousand by January 1st, and then clear sailing: "It's like the first thousand dollars. After you get that the rest comes easier."

But it was that first thousand. Only 130 Model A's were leaving the assembly line daily by January; it was February before every Ford dealer had received at least one sample car. Deliveries that spring were both erratic and slow, so much so that one Ford dealer estimated he had to return about half the deposits made during introductory week, and some deposits were never returned because in the interminable wait the prospective buyers couldn't be relocated. Other dealers who had suffered through the changeover found themselves forced to the wall now. As for prospective buyers, some were lucky, like two Missourians who during Model T days had begun payments for a new Ford from the McGregor Motor Company of Springfield, the first of them having submitted installments of ten cents every time he entered the showroom since 1923, the second—the route manager of a local laundry—having done one of the McGregor salesman's laundry sans bill for two years. By the time the Model A was introduced, they had enough on deposit to secure a Ford. But they were the exceptions. In those early hectic months it was most helpful to have a prominent name in order to get a Model A. Will Rogers—who counted Henry Ford among the men he really liked—was given one of the first ones, a favor he returned by enthusiastically writing the editor of *The New York Times* that since he took to driving it, "nobody is looking at these Rolls-Royces here in Beverly [Hills]." The "Notable Friends of Model A," as the *Ford News* put it, would soon include such luminaries as John D. Rockefeller, Paul Whiteman, Lon Chaney, Louis B. Mayer, Emil Jannings, Wallace Beery, Cecil B. DeMille, Carl Sandburg, Billie Dove, Douglas Fairbanks and Mary Pickford. Prince Nicholas of Rumania was the first in his country to get one. Lillian Gish bought one for her sister Dorothy. Franklin D. Roosevelt told his Poughkeepsie dealer that he took "a great deal of pride in operating" his Model A.

There was a conscious effort on the Ford company's part to get the Model A into the hands of those who wouldn't have laid a velvet glove on the T. The preferential treatment some celebrities received in securing a Model A—a few of them wrote personally to Edsel Ford—did backfire a bit, lesser folk equally as

1931 Mail Truck for U.S. Post Office / Owner: Gary Grebbien

1931 Model 66-A De Luxe Pick-Up

1931 Model 190-A Victoria / Owner: Lawrence Callender

anxious to own a Model A being understandably miffed. The practice was discontinued. Advertised, as it was, amid splendiferous settings of country club chic that would have been equally apropos for one of the three P's, the new low-priced Ford was "positively fashionable," according to Hearst editor Arthur Brisbane. "Everyone who has one is proud of it." More than a few, their appetite whetted, paid extra bonuses to dealers to get one; others receiving an early delivery indulged in a bit of Model A scalping, reselling the car to one of the hungry at a handsome profit. By mid-summer the Model A starvation still hadn't subsided.

It was, as *The Autocar* headlined the problem, that "Mr. Ford [Is] A Human Being, Not A Magician." Naturally in the haste there would be production problems to be ironed out—even Henry Ford couldn't avoid them, and indeed he even contributed to some. His quest for simplicity had, in the case of the Model A's single system brakes, been admirable but the result was soon declared illegal (in the District of Columbia and Pennsylvania) and independent "emergency" or parking brakes were designed into the system by January of 1928. After men and machines were moved around to accommodate the redesign, the production line picked up again. Later during the year the long-favored but now troublesome multi-disc clutch was discarded for a single-plate design. There were other refinements as well, all tending to retard production but finally by November of 1928 Ford's production had climbed to more than 6000 units per day.

It was in November, too, that the five millionth Chevrolet rolled off the assembly line. A month later that General Motors division introduced its 1929 line: six cylinders, six body styles, in a price range of $595 to $725, the lowest priced six-cylinder car in the world. It was the car about which Chevrolet had been thinking since 1925 and to which the company changed over with a minimum of fuss. Only about 120 days had elapsed between discontinuation of the old four and full production capacity for the six. The Model A had been a good year and a half.

Earlier that year a relative newcomer to the manufacturers' ranks, one Walter P. Chrysler, had bought Dodge and presented a new contender in the low-priced field, the Plymouth four.

Which of these two events more concerned Henry Ford—if he was, yet—is not known. Interestingly Europe had the answer, or so thought; rumors swept the Continent by year's end that Ford was planning to unite with Chrysler in all-out battle against General Motors.

Stuff and nonsense. The Model A was sufficiently well received and the Chevrolet sufficiently higher in price for Ford to put up quite a battle all by itself. The Model A's for 1929 were introduced in January, with no announced mechanical changes, but the addition of a number of body styles, including a sprightly cabriolet, town sedan, town car, a variety of new Fordor sedans and a station wagon, the latter the first factory-built station wagon in the industry. Prices had risen to the $435-$670 range (with a hefty $1200 for the elegant town car, $800 for the taxi, also new that year), the increase having been okayed by Henry Ford when it was demonstrated to him early the year previous that on some popular body styles the company was losing money on each unit built. Even the cost-unconscious Henry couldn't ignore that. Nor could he ignore, finally, the entreaties of Joseph Galamb that he (Henry) had gone forge-happy in his approach to the Model A. After Galamb sat first on a piece of forged material, then pressed sheet metal, and neither sagged, Henry was convinced. "That's all right,"

1931 Model A-400 Convertible Sedan / Owner: Dr. Joseph F. Maguire

1931 Model 190-A Victoria / Owner: Bob Paul

1931 Model 35-B Standard Phaeton / Owner: Fred Meyers

1931 Model 55-B Tudor Sedan / Owner: Bud Childress

89

he said—and a shift to malleable castings and stampings for some parts followed. By 1929 producing the Model A had become a profitable enterprise.

By February that year the one millionth Model A was produced; seven months later the two millionth Model A engine was completed. Ford production for 1929 would approach the two-million-unit mark, with Chevrolet second some six hundred thousand units behind. Everybody else was leagues distant from the leaders. Cognizant, obviously, of the encroaching Chevrolet popularity the Ford trade publications began providing its dealers answers to the obvious question. To Murray Fahnestock the Chevrolet slogan, "A Six in the Price Range of the Four," had to mean that it "is not so well built (especially when the six is more pretentious in outside appearance)"—and he proceeded to compare the cars component by component, i.e., the Chevy's thirteen New Departure ball bearings to the Model A's twenty-five from Timken and Hyatt ("Now Timken and Hyatt roller bearings cost real money.") Needless to say, the Chevy fared not at all well.

On October 29th the stock market fared even worse. Henry Ford scarcely heard the crash. In November he reduced prices of some Model A body styles, at the same time raised his workers' wages to a seven-dollar day minimum and on the 19th announced a $60,000,000 building and expansion program. Model A production did decrease in 1930, but it remained as far ahead of Chevrolet as the year previous, and the Ford percentage of the market actually increased from the thirty-five percent of 1929 to forty-two percent.

A higher hood and cowl, new fenders, radiator and hubcaps, new cowl-finish strip and streamline molding, roomier interiors, small wheels with larger tires, and a generous use of chromium and stainless steel characterized the Model A for 1930. Everyone agreed it looked even better than before, including General Motors in a confidential report prepared by its General Technical Committee. Among the new body styles were a deluxe phaeton and victoria coupe. But it was the cabriolet model which the young chief body designer of the Duesenberg company—unable to afford a custom-built Duesenberg—chose that year to redesign into a custom for himself. Gordon Buehrig has since said that the Model A Ford "was probably the highest quality small car ever built."

What was selling the Model A in those days, in addition to its quality and the fact it was a Ford, was advertising, $29,000,000 of it. This was in direct contrast to Model T days, during most of which any ads appearing were courtesy of the dealers. Not for the Model A either was competition viewed as a worthy promotion vehicle. Souped-up A's did appear on dirt tracks across the country, but Ford looked the other way. The Model A's winning of the Courier Race staged by the Delvideki Automobile Club in Szeged ("an important city in Hungary") in 1929 and the Brescia-Ponte di Legno contest in Italy in 1930 was mentioned in the *Ford News*, but not in ads. The only transcontinental trek the Model A took was in celebration of the 20,000,000th Ford produced, in April 1931, the car so designated being driven by Eleanor Roosevelt in New York and Douglas Fairbanks in Los Angeles, with governors, mayors and other worthies signing its log book at various stopping points between the coasts—a far cry indeed from that grimy, mud-flinging treacherous New York-Seattle run two Model T's had taken in 1909, encountering en route prospectors, incredulous farm folk, buffalos and buzzards. It was a long way from the Model T to the Model A.

Henry Ford had in the meantime become an international figure of celebrity and renown. He was indeed as famed and esteemed beyond the borders of the

1931 Model 68-B Convertible Cabriolet / Owner: Ruben L. Nelson

1931½ Model 155 (C or D) Town Sedan / Owner: Randy Siple

1931 Model AF Convertible Saloon by Salmsons & Sons Ltd. / Owner: Harry Hocker

1931 Model 180-A De Luxe Phaeton / Owner: John D. Robertson

United States as he was within them. In Soviet Russia it was proclaimed that he placed second in awe and respect to only one man: Nickolai Lenin. Which was a formidable compliment. Before relations between the two powers turned sour, Henry Ford—like other American corporate magnates—had contributed, via a contract transacted in 1929, to the mechanization of that vast brooding land. He hoped to build a plant in Yugoslavia, but negotiations failed. More promising had been the 1930 proposal for an international combine which would have seen Isotta-Fraschinis built in Detroit, and Fords in Italy, but the Italian government had to approve and ultimately Premier Mussolini didn't. However, Ford enterprises burgeoned in Britain, with a new plant at Dagenham and consolidation of all Ford's Western European interests into the Ford Motor Company Ltd. For a while there were even rumors that Ford might produce a baby car to rival the English varieties—which indeed the company would later do—but at the time this was based on nothing more substantial than the fact that Edsel had bought an M.G. Midget.

What most interested Henry Ford, it can be safely assumed, amid all his endeavors, was the Ford car, and though he grew to like the A very much, it was never more than a summer romance. Even he might have been surprised to learn that of the almost five million Model A's produced an estimated 900,000 survive to this day. Perhaps not, however. Fan letters received by the Ford Motor Company about the car were almost uniformly raves; commendations from law enforcement departments with accounts of thrilling chases in which the Model A police car triumphed over Evil; thank you letters from vacationers relating adventures in which the Model A triumphed over the Sierras. Any faults the Model A had were mentioned almost with apology; if the engine "boiled a little once," that was because "I had the wind behind, and the day was hot"; the vibration at certain speeds was but "a slight rumbling" and "the reliability and the performance of the new Ford are so wonderful that personally I should be perfectly willing to put up with much more noise than the car makes." Particularly welcome were the reports from former six-cylinder car owners who found the Model A "drives and handles more easily, holds the road in a wonderful manner, and is just as smooth and comfortable to ride in. In my judgment . . . in a class all by itself." And Henry Ford must have enjoyed the remarks of the fellow who enthused "when it comes to speed, Oh! Boy! It certainly gets you there. And how!" William Allen White called the Model A "sumptuous" in his Emporia *Gazette.* Present-day owners of Model A Fords wouldn't disagree—in any particular.

The 1931 A was unchanged from the '30, but with the addition of the comely convertible sedan body style. In June that year a jubilant Walter Chrysler had driven over to the Ford plant, with the third example off the line of his new "free wheeling, floating power" Plymouth PA, took Henry and Edsel for a demonstration ride, gave them the car and went home by taxi. That, commented *Fortune* magazine, should give Henry Ford "something to think about." Henry Ford was already thinking about it.

In August 1931, came the announcement of the production shutdown "indefinitely" of the Model A (actually it would be produced through April of 1932). Since late 1929 sporadic rumors had spread of a new model; all had been denied. Now officials simply remained silent about a new car. But there was a lot of talk around that it just might have *eight* cylinders.

INTERREGNUM:
Model B

Everybody was confused. By late fall of 1931, it appeared that another Ford four was in the offing. The company began releasing a flurry of parts orders for what would be called the Model B, but shortly thereafter, in early December, this was followed by stop orders cancelling all deliveries for the time being on most of the components, and unofficial word that Ford would instead build an eight. Still, the trade press advised guardedly that suppliers already hyped for four production need not throw themselves on their order spindles, since the four "according to the latest information available" would be continued for commercial cars and a passenger car version should, God forbid, the competition dare to undersell the new eight. In truth, though no one outside Ford could be certain at the time, the Model B was still on the production schedule—a fact confirmed in early January through further releases by Ford to parts manufacturers for four-cylinder engine components. This brought forth conclusions in automotive journals that the new four would precede the eight into the marketplace. Or at least that Henry Ford might mention it first. There had been no official word at all from the Ford Motor Company as yet about what was going on.

On February 11th, 1932 Henry Ford spoke. And virtually all he could talk about—and with an enthusiasm not seen since his Model T days—was the new Ford eight. "We developed a corking good '4' and were all ready to let it go," he said, "but we found it was not the new effort the public is expecting. That's why we're bringing out the '8' now." It was largely left to other Ford officials to explain that a new four was forthcoming as well, that the flood of letters generated upon rumors of the four's discontinuation had prompted its reinstatement. Enthusiasm for it at Ford, however, was wanting. Apparently some 35,000 of the cars had been built betwixt and between the orders and stop orders, another 50,-000 cars could be built from parts orders now on hand. Yet, when the new Fords were introduced a month and a half later, the poor Model B wasn't even in sight. Only the new V-8's were shown to the five-and-a-half million visitors who crowded into Ford showrooms and exhibitions on that last raucous day in March.

The advertisements for the new line were prophetic: "V-8" ran the headlines and in a small box near the bottom, outlined with the sort of solid black rule usually reserved for death notices, was word of "also an improved 4-cylinder engine." The oh-by-the-way-we've-also-improved-the-four attitude carried forward into press announcements as well; the V-8 in all its glory was described down to the valve head diameters (one and three-eighths inches), while the B was described only as having been refined to deliver 50 hp as opposed to the 40 of its predecessor. This, it was later noted by journalists, was due to the B's higher compression ratio (raised from 4.2 to 4.6 to one), automatic spark advance, heavier crankshaft, polished cylinder walls, larger carburetor and manifold and a change in valve timing, among other refinements.

The Model B was on the same chassis (with a wheelbase of 106 inches as opposed to the A's 103½) and offered substantially the same fourteen body styles as the V-8—and in every case the price was fifty dollars less for the Model B than the V-8. This meant that save for two cases (the phaeton which was ten dollars more and the deluxe coupe which was the same), the Model B sold for fifteen to eighty-five dollars less than the Model A had. But it also worked out that the V-8 was available at a mere twelve fifty more per cylinder. It's scarcely any wonder nobody paid any attention to the Model B.

By late September—a scant six months from its introduction—the trade press was announcing, unofficially of course, that the Model B was being discontinued, this by virtue of the stoppage of releases to parts suppliers in August and the failure to renew the orders when manufacture was resumed at River Rouge after Labor Day. A week later Chris Sinsabaugh in *The New York Times* was echoing the latest Ford rumor—that a six would now become the V-8 companion, apparently forgetting how galling Henry Ford had traditionally found six cylinders. And the rest of the industry speculated "on how strange it would be without a Ford four to compete against." They would find out, though not as soon as rumored. The four-cylinder Model B engine would be an option for Ford passenger cars through 1934. But after the 261,055th Model B was built that year, the four indeed was gone. (The engine, however, would be utilized for light delivery trucks and foreign production until World War II.) Henry Ford was staking everything on his V-8.

THE FORD NOBODY NOTICED

1932 Model B Type 40 Roadster (Standard) / Owner: Dan & Henry Macagni

1932 Model B Type 150 Station W.

ner: John D. Robertson

PART FOUR:
Ford V-8

One could scarcely have imagined him reacting any other way. As the first reverberations of the crash echoed across the land, Henry Ford had cut his prices, raised his wages—and proclaimed cheerful optimism. As the Depression deepened, he would find himself hard put to maintain his first two resolves, he wavered not on the third. Henry Ford was forever sanguine. He was encouraged by the ardent desire of Americans to find work, even as breadlines lengthened. The crash confirmed his distrust of Wall Street. "You can't," he said, "live off a printed bond and a pair of scissors." This proved, the world was now on the threshold of a new and better era; "we are living in the best times," he said in 1933. Even his son Edsel found conditions looking "very, very good" the following year, after offering evidence before a Senate Committee regarding bank losses in Michigan. That year the *New Republic* headlined "Ford Predicts Prosperity." *News Week* declared "Ford Waves Aside Depression," as Henry Ford told the wire services his company, at least, was definitely out of it. Even across the Great Pond, *The Autocar* would look upon Henry Ford's pronouncements as clearly influencing "numerous people to a more optimistic outlook."

There was no question about the power the man wielded. If some intellectuals looked upon him, as H. L. Mencken chided, like "a sort of mixture of Karl Marx and Billy Sunday," most Americans recalled him affectionately, so Will Rogers drawled, "along with Brigham Young [as] the originator of Mass Production . . . who has given us the biggest problem we have in America today, and that is, 'Where am I going to park it?' " The man who had revolutionized the way Americans lived, whose social thinking and practice had elevated the American working man to a dignity of material comfort hitherto unknown had to be listened to. Even as the Thirties, and Henry Ford's reaction to events therein, put some tarnish on the image, he remained in various surveys "the most admired American businessman," among the top four "famous persons" one would like to know, among the five "greatest Americans of all time." Some people—a goodly number of them—still wished him to be President.

All this is intriguing in the extreme, for these were really lamentable years for the Ford Motor Company—and, sad to say, Henry Ford was largely the reason. The grand man was aging. Allusions to this were coming often now. If only Ford himself were properly assembled, one wag said. Still, in 1933 he would be a lively, spry seventy years, with all powers intact, but also with his carefully nurtured prejudices and pertinaciousness more firmly implanted than ever.

The Ford Motor Company had lost over $100 million in 1927 and 1928 (with the T's death and the labor pains concomitant to the A's birth and difficult infant months), had recouped to the pleasant cash register ring of over $91 million profit in 1929, and thereafter fell dismally (along with the rest of industrial America) as the Great Depression spread. Henry Ford's solution was a new baby.

The V-8 was born amid the helter-skelter of what Mencken jocularly called Henry's "great can-factory." Years earlier the Sage of Baltimore had rather neatly summed up the Ford mode of manufacture: "Every afternoon, when work is done, the foremen of each workroom writes down the number of [men] he has had at work during the day and the number of parts he has turned out. Then he divides the latter by the former—and that is his whole report. If the daily figures show a drop, he is called up and ordered to give an account of himself. If they show a rise he gets a note praising him as a competent fellow, and maybe a raise in wages. All such austere and stenographic reports, when they reach the main office in the evening, are put upon an adding machine and added up. If the total today is smaller than yesterday, Ford finds out instantly what shops are at fault. If it is larger, he begins figuring on another cut in the price of flivvers."

Things hadn't changed much at Ford since Model T days. If the administration of production procedures bordered on the fanciful, the engineering setup at Ford might easily have led one to believe serendipity played a part in that aspect of company affairs. Wind tunnels, test tracks, even adequate dynamometer facilities were lacking. Research labs numbered fourteen, but they were scattered, as if to the winds. Centralization was a word seldom heard on the Dearborn plain. Henry Ford was essentially the company's chief engineer—and he

HENRY'S LAST ACT,
THE YEARS OF DRAMA

didn't see the need for such nonsense. His number one engineering lieutenant—and he must be termed thus, since Henry didn't believe in formal titles either—made a stab at sorting out the chaos. But, furtively showing the result to an associate, Laurence Sheldrick cautioned, "Don't let anybody ever see this, because we're not allowed to have an organization chart."

Somehow things got done anyway, and Henry Ford was principally the reason for that as well. Once enthused, he was unstoppable—and the man's uncanny engineering sense was a marvel even to his engineering staff. "Mr. Ford reads a machine the way a bibliophile reads a first edition," one of their number said. Another swore that if six identical carburetors were placed in a row, five good, one bad, Henry Ford could pick out the errant one just by looking at them. Almost to a man, however, they would have preferred that he stay away sometimes. Certain ideas he could not countenance: hydraulic brakes, longitudinal springs, Hotchkiss drive—anything, some would later say, that GM or Chrysler tried first. But neither Chrysler nor GM nor anyone else for that matter were about to come up with a low-priced V-8—and that's precisely what Henry Ford had in mind. Wanting to improve [read modernize] Henry's basic V-8 idea in later years, Edsel Ford and Charles Sorensen managed to remove production engineering from Dearborn to new headquarters in the Rouge where, as Laurence Sheldrick put it, "He couldn't pop in so often. . . ."

Henry Ford would allow the transfer then probably because his Greenfield Village, his devotion to the soy bean and its multitude of uses, his village industries plan all weighed heavily on his time. But during the development of the V-8, he was "the dynamo of the works," as reporter James Sweinhart wrote at the time, turning up "here, there, everywhere, ordering, directing, changing."

Whether a six-cylinder engine played a significant part in post Model A plans is problematical. Apparently some experimental work had been done, though Henry Ford wasn't overly enthused. He thought generally in fours and multiples thereof—experimental eights, twelves, even an X-shaped twenty-four purportedly being run up in Ford labs during the Twenties. His mind was made up in 1929,

1932 Model 18 Type 68 Cabriolet / Henry Ford Museum

1932 Model 18 Type 520 Coupe (De Luxe) / Owner: Gary & Henry Macagni

with GM's help. "We're going from a four to an eight," he told engineering assistant Fred Thoms, "because Chevrolet is going to a six." Thoms was ordered to "get all the eight-cylinder engines that you can." The order was, of course, quickly carried out. He managed to buy, or otherwise procure, nine of them.

His father, Edsel Ford said, was "never happier than when he is solving some big mechanical problem" or directing efforts toward his personal truism that "the fewer the parts, the less the risk of trouble." "A bolt," he mused, "shows two things joined that, perhaps should be one thing." He wasn't enamored of welds either. The various eight-cylinder engines Thoms had gathered for his perusal were dusted off and laid out in a line. Each one was built of up segments numbering two or three. Too many parts, Henry said, too costly. A single, solid, rigid block was necessary. It couldn't be done, everybody said. It could, Henry said. It would be.

"So I went back to my old trade of patternmaking," production chief Sorensen remembered later, and received from Joe Galamb "a layout that I could adapt to our Rouge foundries." He worked long and hard. Henry helped. The story is told that when casting problems arose, he simply happened by the foundry one day with a bundle under his arm, changed into overalls and got to work. "You can't solve these things by paper work," he always said. "You have got to see them."

The foundry revamping would result in further advances in the manufacture of cast steel for components previously forged, this resulting in savings of time and cost, and greatly increased strength and durability. Ford's development of the cast alloy crankshaft was hailed by *Automotive Industries* in 1936 as "one of the most important contributions to automotive engineering in recent years." While it is true—as deriders incessantly point out—that the Thirties saw Ford less a leader than a follower in engineering advances, this tends to ignore what a good idea the Ford V-8 engine was, how nice a unit it became and the many lessons its manufacture taught. This is mentioned early, because carrying the story forward through its years in the marketplace will only too obviously detail what the V-8 lacked.

In May of 1930 the first experimental engine had been completed, in November the second; two or two-and-a-half dozen more followed. For secrecy's sake, the work had begun in the old Edison laboratory which Henry Ford brought to Greenfield Village from Fort Myers, Florida, with preliminary drawings sketched on "Lincoln" drafting paper. Thomas Edison was among the first of Henry's friends to ride around in one of the prototype V-8's. It was spring 1931. Refinement continued. Now the principal question became one of timing—not the engine's, but the car's production.

The initial decision was that the time was not right, business conditions were too unstable to bring out the eight. An improved Model A might be a better idea—and they could call it the Model B. Work was frantically begun on it, under the watchful eye of Henry Ford. By late fall 1931, it was in production. The plant was humming smoothly, but as one of his workers said, "[Mr. Ford's] old smile didn't come back," as it usually did on such occasions. "Instead, somehow, he seemed to be getting madder and madder." The conclusion: "We knew he felt we weren't yet on the right track." But that was solved the morning of December 7th when the Fords, father and son, met together in Edsel's offices in the Dearborn laboratories. An hour later the V-8 was back on the calendar.

This obviously presented a problem, seeing as the assembly lines were full of Model B's. One is reminded of those hysterical stop-the-presses scenes in newspaper dramas of the period. A production halt was quickly ground to, machinery was uprooted, its place taken by quickly designed, rapidly contracted

1932 Model 18 Type 35 Phaeton (Standard) / Owner: Arthur Ahlstone

for and hurriedly installed new machines for the V-8. Word was passed about on all this, and it resulted in a flood of letters to Ford begging for the four to be continued. Henry backtracked a bit, reinstated half his work force to the Model B endeavor, and together with the other half, he himself began the gargantuan task of preparing the V-8 for immediate production. Of where his enthusiasm lay, there was no doubt.

"I've just got my old determination back. That's all," Henry confided to newsman Sweinhart. It was February 11th, 1932 — and the *Detroit News* reporter was the first officially to announce the answer to the question "the whole automobile world has been asking . . . since the Spring of 1930." When asked, Henry alluded to the four, and modestly demurred that an eight was, after all, just two fours put together. But there was no hiding the twinkle in his eye. News of the forthcoming low-priced V-8 made every important paper in the United States the next day. Its first public showing was scheduled for early March.

Laid to rest now were all the old rumors about what Ford was going to do — these having been so hot and heavy that the *New York Post* suspected "a rumor-for-the-week-idea" had been launched, presumably by Ford. One week in the summer of 1932 a particularly tantalizing one, reported in the *Bergen Evening Record*, noted that the company was planning a V-8 diesel-engined car, about which Ford, as usual, had no comment, but certainly no real interest either.

Fresh rumors now replaced the stale, some of them a bit more reliable. "Industry Awaits Zero Hour As Ford Rumors Are Blasted" declared *Automotive Industries* on February 20th, and its editors allowed that speculation regarding the new eight now remained only on price, effect on market, dimensional details of the cars and actual date of first showing. Henry Ford "is the master of the art of suspense," concluded the *Toronto Financial Post*.

Announcement a week earlier that Ford planned to reemploy 30,000 men for the V-8 effort was regarded by financial and industrial leaders as the biggest piece of news since the "business illness" began some two years earlier. Alvan Macauley and Roy D. Chapin, among others, were queried — and they said they thought what Henry Ford was doing was just grand. Frank Knox, chairman of President Hoover's Citizens Reconstruction Organization to End Hoarding, used his paper *(The Daily News)* to laud the industrialist for his vigorous "attack on hard times." A Massachussets journal gushed that Henry Ford was "an American Moses leading his people out of the Land of Depressed Bondage into a new economic Land of Promise." As for Ford himself, he was prepared, he said, to "risk all," spending hundreds of millions to build 1,500,000 cars in 1932, realizing that his manufacturing alone would not end the Depression, but "you know, faith is catching."

By early March the new V-8 had not shown up — and, while newspapers headlined the tragedy of the Lindbergh baby kidnapping, on the 7th it was reported, from gossip emanating from Youngstown, Ohio, that mechanical difficulties had arisen. Four days later the word was that the first of the new models had been completed, two days after that rumor had it that Detroit manufacturers of competitively priced cars might suspend operations until the V-8 was on the market.

The latter was patently ridiculous. With the announcement that the new V-8 would appear, finally, on the last day in March, Walter Chrysler for one got himself ready. In full-page ads four days before the event, he appeared, his arm casually flung over the headlight of his new Plymouth (the only part of the car showing, the rest would come April 2nd), confirming the "Important Rumor" that Plymouth would be fighting for the lowest-priced market and talking in

1933 Model 40 Type 720 Coupe (De Luxe) / Owner: Bob Kennedy

1933 Model 40 Type 710 Roadster (De Luxe) / Owner: Nick Cassaro

1933 Model 40 Type 700 Sedan (De Luxe) / Owner: Robert B. Flaner

capital letters of Free Wheeling, Floating Power, Hydraulic Brakes, Safety Steel Body, Automatic Clutch. On March 31st another full-page ad showed Chrysler and a bit more of the Plymouth, the former's foot on the latter's bumper, his hand fondling its radiator ornament. "Look At All Three," he exhorted, just a mite snidely adding, "It is my opinion that any new car without Patented Floating Power is obsolete."

That day 5,501,952 people across the country got a look at the new Ford including — so the story goes — an on-duty streetcar motorman who, seeing a tarpaulin-covered object being driven into a dealer's garage early that morning, shut off the current and hied himself thereto, followed by his conductor and passengers. Prior to the opening, deposits on orders for some 100,000 Fords (only twenty-five percent of them the new fours) had been placed; another 100,000 came in the few days after the introduction, most of these being for the V-8, the Model B not having been shown. *The New York Times* closed its report of the V-8's Broadway debut (1740 Broadway, to be exact) with, "undetermined is the date when deliveries will begin in this city." It was rather in the nature of a prophecy.

Within forty-eight hours Detroit reported that the rest of the industry had begun to "move at a feverish pace reminiscent of those climactic days of '29." None of his competitors would be conceding Ford the bulk of the business that had been deferred pending arrival of the new cars. In their absence the competition had been fighting "against a phantom whose very mystery gave it a phenomenal appeal." Now the fight was out in the open. The combatant had arrived at last.

And what was it, this new car from Ford, designated Model 18, "8" for the number of cylinders, "1" because it was the first eight produced by Ford. First the engine: a 90° flathead with special heat treated aluminum alloy pistons; sixty-five-pound counterweighted crankshaft; compression ratio of 5.5 to one; three main bearing camshaft, valves with mushroom ends requiring no adjustment; connecting rods of single-end type mounted side by side on the crankpins and riding in long-life babbitt-backed bearings; downdraft carburetor; tube and fin radiator; full pressure lubrication; a cooling system combining both pump and thermosyphon; rubber engine mountings. With cylinders, crankcase and flywheel housing cast in a single unit, making possible a short, rigid crankshaft, the Ford V-8 engine required no more space in the car than a four. With bore-stroke dimensions of 3-1/16 by 3¾ for 221 cubic inches and 65 bhp, its horsepower per cubic inch was the most meritorious of sixteen cars in the low and medium price range. And its power to weight ratio was extraordinarily high. Henry Ford liked light cars, and the V-8 was undoubtedly that, at about 2500 pounds, some 600 to 700 pounds lighter than the Oldsmobile, Pontiac and Willys eights and lighter than nearly all the four- and six-cylinder cars in the $1000 price class. It could do a genuine 75 mph.

But that's getting ahead of the specifications: torque tube drive; single plate clutch and three-speed selective sliding type transmission with synchronized second and third gears and a silent helical cut constant mesh gear in second speed; I-beam front axle, rear three-quarter floating; transverse cantilever springs front and rear; self-adjusting Houdaille double acting hydraulic shock absorbers with thermostatic control; chassis and running gear cushioned by rubber insulators in spring shackles and shock absorber links; fully enclosed four wheel mechanical brakes with 186 square inches of braking area; electrically welded one-piece steel spoke wheels; double drop frame; all steel bodies insulated from frame by rubber pads; shatterproof glass windshield and windshield wings; fourteen body styles —

1934 Model 40 Type 740 Victoria / Owner: Bob Kennedy

1934 Model 40 Type 750 Ph

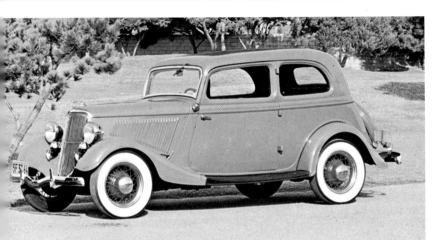

1934 Model 40 Type 740 Victoria / Owner: Dick Holland

...uxe) / Owner: Mori Nelson

all of them save the phaeton designed by LeBaron, the phaeton probably having fallen together under the aegis of Edsel Ford, Joe Galamb and the people at Briggs. The price range: $460-$650, as compared to the Model A's $430-$640.

That's what the V-8 Ford had. Let's look now at what it hadn't. A long wheelbase, for one thing. This dimension wasn't even initially mentioned. When newsmen had asked at a private showing at the plant, Ford officials said only that it "was not an indication of the real size and roominess of the car," that owing to special body construction passengers in the new car would have considerably more space than in the Model A. All very true, certainly, but it was also true that the Ford V-8 was shorter in wheelbase than fifteen of its sixteen competitors in the under $1000 price class. Only the Terraplane shared its 106-inch dimension; the Plymouth, for example, was 112, Chevrolet 109.

Murray Fahnestock, writing in the *Ford Dealer & Service Field*, tried to turn this into an advantage: "all the other cars . . . have a clumsier wheelbase than the Ford. . . . What's the last piece of apparatus to arrive at a fire? The hook-and-ladder truck, which, because of its long wheelbase, is heavy and ungainly and cannot take turns at high speed." He was straining a bit there, but he mounted a stern offense in proclaiming the Ford's torque tube drive superior to "the old-fashioned 'Hotchkiss' drive," and a stout defense in praising the retention of Ford's patented transverse springs: "Although these patents have now expired, it would be very embarrassing for any other manufacturers to now copy a type of spring suspension so prominently identified as Ford." His associate Thomas Howe, ignoring the hydraulics of the Plymouth, commented that Ford's mechanical brakes were the same type as used on Cadillac, LaSalle, Lincoln, Marmon, Packard and Pierce-Arrow. (Ford advertised "the safety of steel from toe to wheel!") The absence of free wheeling and an automatic clutch was alluded to in a *New York Times* article: "it is said to have been Henry Ford's intention to make the car as simple in construction as possible, and engineers have not convinced him of the desirability of incorporating these features in the new car."

Actually the Ford Motor Company was having sufficient problems coping with just what it had. The hurry into production had presented its logistical difficulties, and the V-8, as splendid an idea as it was, had teething problems of its own. Heads cracked, piston rings leaked, oil consumption was prodigious, ignition was faulty, the engine mounts vibrated loose. The original location of the water pump in the cylinder head, at Henry Ford's insistence, meant, as Laurence Sheldrick explained, that "you were trying to pull hot water out of the engine at the top rather than push cold water in at the bottom." This was solved in 1937 by relocation of the pump "on the entrance side of the system" where the water came into the block. Remedies for most of the other complaints were sooner forthcoming. Still, some damage had been done. Production hobbled to 212,057 units for 1932, about fifteen percent of Ford's optimistic forecast. And, for the 1933 season, the Ford Motor Company, traditionally opposed to the yearly model change, had one all its own. It would be the first of many. In the late winter of 1932 Henry Ford had his appendix out. One wonders how he found the time.

The "long awaited new Ford" — it was delayed, and that was now almost becoming a tradition — was introduced the second week in February 1933. It was designated Model 40, and immediately noticeable was its length. The hook-and-ladder rationale notwithstanding, the Ford was now six inches longer in wheelbase, or 112 inches. It also had an entirely new frame, double drop with a stiffening X-member; the rear axle was strengthened, rubber engine mounts improved, the radiator made larger. By use of aluminum alloy cylinder heads with redesigned combustion chambers, power of the V-8 was raised to 75 hp at 3800 rpm for a sustained speed capability of 80 mph. It was the most powerful Ford built since the company began volume production — and notwithstanding that one is always open to argument on such conclusions, the prettiest as well. Edsel Ford had been the company's president for more than a decade now, albeit with little of the authority the title would imply. By this time, however, he was allowed a virtually free hand in styling, a wise decision on Henry's part, although it must be admitted the elder Ford was never particularly interested in style anyway. The first V-8's were pleasantly designed essentially in the Model A mode, the new cars were a graceful departure: sweeping lines carried to the sloping windshield and skirted fenders; radiator grille angled deftly to that of the windshield, the rear lines of the hood and the forward edge of the door; new acorn-shaped headlamps; full-bar bumpers — a lovely package all around. Interestingly, the design was really a magnification of the small 1933-1934 British Fords built at Dagenham which E. T. "Bob" Gregorie had drawn up at Edsel's request in 1932. So impressed was Edsel with the result that it was applied to the new U.S. Ford too. By 1935 Gregorie, who had joined the company in 1931, would create and take charge of Ford's first styling department, working closely always with Edsel Ford. Edsel, though not a designer himself, was a superb critic with an eye for line and detail and style that was as uncanny as his father's mechanical knack. He and Gregorie were kindred spirits; "we appreciated each other," Gregorie said.

Ford had lost some $44 million in 1932, though the company was hardly alone in failing to turn a profit. As the full force of the Depression was beginning to be felt throughout America, Henry Ford remained of good cheer. Nineteen thirty-three promised to be better. Ford writers who had taken pains during the Model A era to demonstrate the advantages of the four- over the six-cylinder engine, now turned to hymning the superiority of a V-8 over a six or an in-line eight. The company itself had the selling job, as *Fortune* put it, of convincing Depression buyers that an eight wouldn't necessarily use more fuel than a six nor would it shake the car to pieces. Yet, with the kinks worked out of the V-8 engine and a new and much improved model, this loomed as a not insurmountable task.

Meanwhile Franklin Delano Roosevelt had been elected President of the United States. "Drive Right In, Frank," enthused *Ford Dealer & Service Field*, "park your car and take your place at the executive desk of this great Nation." The publication was *not* affiliated with the Ford Motor Company. At the very beginning, however, Henry Ford shared the sentiment and was pleasantly effusive in his belief that the new President would put the country right again. Then, on June 16th, 1933, FDR signed the National Industrial Recovery Act, with its provisions for self regulation by American industry as to maximum work hours, minimum pay rates, production quotas and, under Section 7A, the right of labor to organize. Henry was livid. A week later a Ford advertisement appeared throughout the country wherein the industrialist noted the eight-hour day, the five-day week, a minimum wage that always exceeded the market rate, the "industrial decencies [Ford had achieved] not by regulation or compulsion." The ad, *Automotive Industries* commented shortly thereafter, "is being interpreted in some quarters as an indication that Mr. Ford is opposed to any governmental interference in his business." That was putting it mildly. "Proud and glad to do our part" was the Chevrolet slogan, the NRA flag flew above the factories turning out Plymouths, but to Henry Ford the Blue Eagle was "Roosevelt's Buzzard." He wasn't about to sign the automobile code devised at the behest of the government by the National Automobile Chamber of Commerce. He had stood his ground alone once before — in the Selden Patent case. He was a lone wolf, a maverick again. It was entirely in character. Henry Ford was a Populist, and

1934 Model 40 Type 860 Station Wagon / Owner: Craig Clemens

1934 Model 40 Type 720 Coupe (De Luxe) Owner: Dave Ruesch

1934 Model Y Saloon De Luxe, English / Owner: James A. Crawford

1934 Model 40 Type 730 Sedan (De Luxe) / Owner: Mori Nelson

Populism, although reformist and philosophically left of the political spectrum, avidly endorsed free competition. But Henry had a simple solution anyway, as summed up in the title of a *Christian Century* article: "Mr. Ford Will Obey But He Will Not Enlist." His decision to follow the automobile code without accepting it, alas, did not sit well in Washington. But neither the administration's attacks on Ford nor the directive that the government would not buy products of non-compliant firms moved Henry Ford. Though it did move much of America to a favorable stance squarely behind the industrialist. As Will Rogers said, "you can take the rouge from female lips, the cigarettes from the raised hands, the hot dogs from the tourists' greasy paws, but when you start jerking the Fords out from under the traveling public you are monkeying with the very fundamentals of American life." And the Kansas City *Journal Post* asked how the public could penalize a man who years previous developed the basic humanitarian ideas of NRA and put them into practice merely because he failed to sign up to do that which he was already doing. The question really answered itself. President Roosevelt appreciated Ford's viewpoint. The two men exchanged birthday cards. Eventually a poultry manufacturer named Schechter and the Supreme Court would combine to destroy the NRA, and Henry Ford could cease refusing his signature.

Wily old Henry even pulled a public relations coup out of the entire situation. Always ill at ease when making speeches — he frequently joked that the first speech he ever gave was at Sing Sing and his opening line was "I'm glad to see you all here" — he took the occasion of the announcement of the 1934 Ford line to broadcast a statement via telephone hookup to his 24,000 American and Canadian dealers and salesmen. "We have all got to pitch in and do all the business we can," he said, "to help the President pull the country out of the hole." This, in the midst of the Ford-NRA contretemps, made front page headlines across the country — and coincidentally was a rather effective advertisement for the new Ford line of automobiles.

Significantly, *Automotive Industries* noted that the new Ford was introduced "without any abnormal interruption in production" — a break in recent company tradition. And the new Model 40 would be sold as "The Car Without a Price Class," the copy stressing Ford features to be found only in higher-priced cars. Engine improvements, early in 1934, included a new dual downdraft carburetor and dual intake manifold which combined to increase power by about twelve percent, push the maximum speed up to 87 mph and concomitantly result in an additional two to three miles per gallon. (The new car gave 20 mpg at 45 mph in company conducted tests.) The crankshaft was now cast rather than forged, and there was a new body ventilator system operated by individual controls on front door and rear quarter windows. Outside, a new radiator contour, longer hood and shorter cowl dominated the styling changes. Underneath, the V-8 remained much the same.

Chevrolet, of course, had adopted independent front suspension for '34, which left Ford to explain its adherence to the principle of the transverse spring. "Because it retains the important advantages of the solid axle and yet minimizes road shocks transmitted to frame and body," said company engineers. Henry Ford put it even more succinctly: "We use transverse springs for the same reason that we use round wheels — because we have found nothing better for the purpose." *Ford Dealer & Service Field* pooh-poohed, " 'Knees'? No, Thank You."

"Can a champion come back?" asked *Advertising and Selling.* Well, not completely, not this champion. In 1934 Ford turned a profit ($3,759,311), the first time since 1930; and in 1935 more Fords were sold than any other make, also the

1935 Model 48 Type 760 Cabriolet / Owner: Bob Wilson

first time since 1930. But the days of Ford's dominance of the industry were gone. In 1936 the Ford car slipped back to number two behind the Chevrolet; and the company slid to number three behind Chrysler and General Motors. GM, of course, marketed six cars, Chrysler four, Ford but two.

It was, as Will Rogers said, that Henry Ford "broke in more customers for other cars than necessity." And they were buying them now more than ever. Henry Ford's various attitudes and poses — all widely reported — had alienated some markets. His aversion to cigarettes and liquor made Ford salesmen less than popular to tobacco manufacturers and breweries for their fleet sales. (Curiously, Henry offered beer and cigarettes to newsmen at the preview for the '34 models, and this made almost as much news as the cars.) The more dedicated of New Dealers obviously weren't Ford fanciers, nor were many Jewish Americans who recalled the infamous Shapiro case of the Twenties and who would be further dismayed by what was purportedly seen to be pro-Nazi sentiment on Henry Ford's part in the late Thirties. By that time, too, Henry's attitude toward unions would disaffect yet another segment of the market.

Although liberation had not yet become part of the woman's lexicon, one wonders if Henry might not have disenchanted some of that vast group with his comments that women would disappear from industry because "they do not want to think on mechanical and industrial matters, and, as a matter of fact, do not want to think much about anything." But he wanted them to buy his cars. In 1934 the Ford Motor Company opened a women's automobile salon in the Kern department store in Detroit with the object of proving that the modern car was not "too complicated for women to understand." An ad for the 1939 model showed a wife exclaiming, "Oh, Darling! It's so lovely that I haven't a thing to go with it" — while her husband looked on, near catatonia. Poor Henry, even in trying to appeal to women, he came off decidedly sexist. But then so did most everyone else in those days.

Yet, what was not selling Fords truly was not Henry Ford but the cars themselves. America had cottoned to the idea of such things as hydraulic brakes and independent front suspension, and the Ford's lack of both — while the competition boldly touted same — was damaging. The V-8's admirable performance qualities appealed to the likes of John Dillinger and Clyde Barrow, both of whom wrote Henry Ford regarding their preference for Fords, but more and more Americans were demanding the advantages of engineering sophistication and further creature comforts.

Indeed it can be fairly said that England was far more appreciative of the V-8 than the United States ever was. Upon its introduction the venerable Scribe of *The Autocar* spent a "thrilling" weekend with one, "an astounding experience which no words can adequately describe . . . I have been in other cars with similar powers but they have been of the sports type, and acceleration has been synonymous with noise and tremor. The Ford V-8 engine never lets you know it is under the bonnet; somehow, one subconsciously places it at the rear, for the car seems to be swept along *before* a giant hand and not pulled along by machinery." Though *The Autocar* complained mildly that the brakes groaned a bit and might have been better, they actually liked the transverse suspension, finding it the equal of some independently sprung systems.

But what really set English hearts aflutter is perhaps best summarized by tributes paid in *The Autocar* road tests of the V-8 through those years: "a car with a performance up to nearly 80 m.p.h. that can be equalled by very few machines on the road to-day, even by those of sports type . . . it is . . . all that can possibly be wanted" (1932); "the rapidity with which the car would get up to 55 or 60 m.p.h.

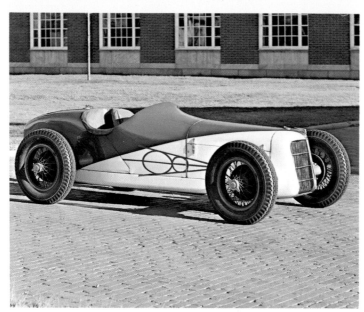

1935 Miller-Ford Indianapolis race car / Henry Ford Museum

1935 Model 48 Type 770 Coupe (Standard) / Owner: John L. Jefferson

in a smooth, quiet sweep, without the slightest hesitation was indeed a fascinating part of its behaviour" (1933); "not only has the V8 such a performance on the gears that the ordinary sports car can comfortably be left, but on top gear, too, the ability to pick-up is astonishingly good" (1934); "anyone who had not had previous experience of a car of this description could but be astounded by the ease of the running at 40 to 50 m.p.h. . . . and by the way in which the speedometer needle literally shoots across the dial" (1935); "starting was very quick at all times, and the car could be driven away almost at once" (1936); "there is the very satisfactory feeling of its possessing a great reserve of power, so that the engine is seldom fully extended on ordinary roads" (1937); "fast driving and severe use of the gears leave the engine untroubled afterwards" and "equally, it is a pleasant car for pottering" (1938); "almost any normal hill where there is an opportunity to keep the car running fairly briskly on the approach is climbable on top gear . . . there is not the slightest question of its being necessary to rush ordinary main road gradients in order to climb them on top gear" (1939). In 1934 a V-8 saloon did 0-50 in 10-3/5 seconds (a second slower than the twelve-cylinder Hispano-Suiza also tested that year), 0-60 in 16-4/5 seconds (a second slower than the 4½-liter Lagonda). Very little else could stay with it. A Studebaker Dictator, for example, was a full ten seconds slower. In 1938 a V-8 was timed at 87.38 mph on the Brooklands track.

Little wonder that Edsel Ford, on a trip to England, wistfully told the Scribe that he read *The Autocar* every week and wished America had a journal like it. The letters column of the magazine frequently showed correspondence from readers getting "excited about the excellence of these cars" — and the goings-on of the chummy Ford Enthusiasts' Club (begun in 1938) were regularly reported: the Ford enclosure at the Donington Grand Prix that year, the trials, the contests, the runs. One British Ford dealer, Sydney Allard made quite a name — and a business — for himself with his V-8's and the equally formidable trials specials he made thereof.

Elsewhere in the world the V-8 was making itself known too. Early sporting victories included two by women — though Henry Ford probably didn't notice — Madame A. Dassier winning the ten-kilometer race on Ford Day at Hanoi, French Indo-China in 1932, and Samiye Burhan Djahit Hanim bettering her closest competitor by seventeen minutes in a race at Istanbul in 1933. More significant was the six-year monopoly of open road racing that the V-8 enjoyed in Brazil. And the phenomenal success in the Monte Carlo Rally. Starting off modestly in 1935 with Mme. Marinovitch and Mlle. Lamberjack winning the Ladies Cup, accelerating in 1936 when P.G. Cristea and I. Zamfirescou won outright (second was taken by the Delahaye driven by the husband-wife Schell team, parents of Harry) and sixteen of the twenty-six Fords entered finished, falling off the mark in 1937 with a seventh place by Cristea, the V-8 record in the event was capped in 1938 with twenty-six cars entered, the rally won by G. Bakker Schut and Karel Ton, and the capturing of no fewer than eighteen other cups by V-8's. No other car before or since can boast a similar success.

But that was as child's play compared to the V-8's sporting record in America. If racing success had sold cars in this country, Henry Ford couldn't have built his V-8's fast enough. They were simply phenomenal. It all began at the Elgin National Road Race for stock cars on August 26th, 1933. Fords swept the first seven places, Fred Frame (the previous year's Indy winner) winning at 80.22 mph. One spectator was quoted in a Ford trade publication as commenting, "It was an enlightening demonstration of the road-holding ability achieved by Ford's transverse springs and the resulting low unsprung weight, the torque tube drive,

1935 Model 48 Type 750 Phaeton / Owner: Jeff Millevick

and the double acting Houdaille shock absorbers. This combination carried the weight, and was not bothered in the least by the transmission of the remarkable V-8 zip and power." One might suspect some of the words having been put in his mouth — but not the sentiment. On February 24th, 1934, Stubby Stubblefield led nine other Fords to a ten-car sweep of the Gilmore Gold Cup race at the Los Angeles Municipal Airport; on Labor Day B. P. Hammond, Angelo Cimino and Glen Schultz shattered all stock car records to take the first three places in the climb up Pikes Peak.

It should be said that most of the cars entered in these events were Ford V-8's, but that was telling in itself. The hepped-up enthusiasm with which Ford dealers jumped to enter such contests — with the company's blessing and encouragement — was matched by the dour reluctance of Ford's competitors to do the same. Indeed most manufacturers warned their dealers not to accept the many Ford challenges flung their way. To take on a V-8 was absurd.

Road racing had virtually died in this country after the First World War, but the Automobile Racing Club of America revived it in the Thirties on twisting circuits at Cape Cod, Briarcliff, Alexandria Bay, Montauk and elsewhere, its corps of enthusiastic amateurs providing the spark that would explode after the Second World War into sports car racing as we know it today. The flathead V-8, and the Model B engine too, played an often overlooked but important role during this interim period, both being stuffed into numerous sporting specials and foreign chassis (once the original engines gave out). The club's winningest car was the Old Gray Mare which had seen in turn a Model T, Model A and V-8 engine cradled between its frame rails. Leo Levine, in his excellent book, *Ford: The Dust and the Glory*, suggested that Ford power was perhaps a factor as instrumental as any other in forming the basis of the sport as we know it today. The suggestion, a bold one, is not without merit. His argument is impressive. But so then was the V-8 Ford.

Not so impressive was the V-8 at Indianapolis. In 1933 hometown dealer C. O. Warnock's V-8 Ford was the slowest car to try to qualify: In 1934 Charles Crawford finished sixteenth (110 laps) and Chet Miller was accorded thirty-third place, dropping out on the eleventh lap. Then Preston Tucker had an idea. To make a long, sad story as brief as possible, Tucker proposed teaming up with Harry Miller and the Ford Motor Company for an all-out ten-car assault on the 500; Edsel liked the idea, Henry didn't, but was convinced around February of 1935; a deal was done, Ford was to provide Miller-Tucker — through its advertising agency, N. W. Ayer & Son — with $25,000 worth of V-8 engines, parts and services, a figure later upped to $75,000; the borrowed machinery and equipment arrived at Miller-Tucker on March 12th; Tucker promoted — did he ever promote! — and came up with a team of top-notch drivers headed by Peter DePaolo; Miller worked day and night with his crew to build the first front-wheel-drive, four-wheel-independent-suspension cars ever to appear at Indianapolis; the cars dribbled into the Speedway from May 12th to May 25th; DePaolo tried the first car in practice on May 15th and complained of steering difficulties, "don't worry, you just drive it," he was told; qualifying began May 19th, three cars weren't ready, two failed to qualify, one qualified only as an alternate; four of the cars started the 500, all dropped out with steering maladies, Ted Horn's after 360 miles, good for sixteenth place, the best finish for the team. Simply put, the project was an admirable example of what haste makes. "The best looking, best streamlined cars ever seen at the Speedway" — so *Motor* said — were so hurriedly constructed that mechanical deficiencies were ignored. And some $42,244 was spent above the contracted figure. Henry Ford was furious.

His company would thereafter forget about racing for a decade and a half.

Indianapolis hadn't done the company a power of promotional good, and though racing was alluded to in some advertising, it would appear Ford was happier in promoting the qualities of the car as evidenced in the many endurance runs and trials conducted with the V-8. These were sponsored sometimes by newspapers, more often by oil companies, as for example the thirty-three days race driver Eddie Pullen and his crew spent traveling 33,000 miles in the Mojave Desert with a V-8 for Pennzoil. Ford publications regularly touted the extensive treks taken by Ford owners as well, including Ethel Hueston, author of some twenty successful novels, "including the much loved *Prudence of the Parsonage*," who packed her husband, Randolph Blinn, and her German shepherd, Fraulein Frieda von Hueblin, into a V-8 and traveled 14,000 miles cross country to gather material for her next historical novel. It was a marvelous trip, Miss Hueston commented, "without backache, headache or heartache." She did have a way with words.

Ford also inaugurated an "Oddities . . . with apologies to Ripley" column, relating the more curious experiences owners had with V-8's: a fellow in Beaumont, California chasing a large wolf across the desert until he ran it down with his, another gentleman in Bathe, Ohio carrying a snowman twenty-five miles on the running board of his. Although not as extensively as had been done with the Model A, Ford also made note of celebrities and other interesting owners of V-8's: Wallace Beery, Buster Keaton, Louis B. Mayer, Bobby Jones, Buddy Rogers, "famed Mexican" General Pascual Ortiz Rubio (the country's former president) and the ex-king of Spain, Alfonso XIII, whose fondness for Hispano-Suizas was legendary. His Royal Highness Prince Monnireth of Cambodia and Polish Minister (the son of the President of the Republic of Poland) His Excellency, Michael Moscicki had V-8's, and Prince Knud and Princess Mathilde of Denmark took their honeymoon in theirs. Among V-8 owners also were Goodyear balloonist Ward T. Van Orman, Sheriff F. M. Wheeler of Baraboo, Wisconsin, and a number of gentlemen noteworthy for their heft — apparently 350 pounds or thereabouts was the qualifying minimum — variously described as the "largest grocer in the state" or the "South's largest turpentine operator." But most noted of V-8 drivers certainly were Charles Lindbergh and, when he found the opportunity, President Roosevelt. While governor of New York, the latter had been an enthusiastic Model A owner, though now he probably spent many more of his motoring hours in the official Presidential Lincoln.

Music — a favored Henry Ford pastime — was much a part of V-8 promotion as well, Eugene's Magyar Tzigane's Band, Medvedeff's Balalaika Orchestra, and Troise and his Mandoliers and Banjoliers serenading at Ford exhibitions at the Royal Albert Hall in London — and King Palmer organizing what was believed to be the first musical group ever named after a car; the V8 Shadow Symphony Orchestra. In America Arthur Murray had college youngsters dancing "The V-8 Chassis Swing."

All this, of course, was no substitute for an effective advertising program, but here N. W. Ayer & Son had Henry to contend with — and Henry was not favorably disposed. "If advertising is to be like a bouquet which a business pins upon itself," he said, "it might just as well be left off." Ford advertising was conservative and, as *Fortune* said, unoriginal and unimpressive also. A massive direct mail campaign in 1933 was described as a "message of intelligent buying, an educational endeavor." The 1935 model might be described as the best car the Ford company ever built, but not the best car period — Henry wouldn't allow that. "Don't exaggerate," he would caution, "the truth is big enough." When the

1936 Model 68 Type 700 Tudor Sedan (De Luxe) / Owner: Jim Spero

1936 Model 68 Type 780 Sedan Delivery / Owner: John Ryan

1936 Model 68 Type 750 Phaeton / Owner: William H. Sutton

1936 Model 68 Type 740 Convertible Sedan / Owner: Ollie Smith

1936 Model 68 Type 760 Club Cabriolet / Owner: R.H. Verner

1936 Model 68 Type 790 Station Wagon / Owner: Joe Price, Jr.

competition in some localities became rather pointed in critical references to Ford, Henry replied with large ads stating, "There are some things we refuse to do to sell a car." A rare example of company coyness came with the advertisement titled "America Sees the Big Three of '41" — featuring the Lincoln, the Mercury, the Ford.

In advertising volume for the period, Ford trailed both General Motors and Chrysler, but it is doubtful that increased expenditures would have altered the Ford situation significantly. Although Henry Ford patented a rear-engined car in 1936, he mitigated its importance as "merely one of many engineering developments of our research" — and perhaps justifiably, since aggressive engineering was not finding its way into the production V-8. LeBaron designed a seven-passenger sedan and limousine which were introduced by New Era Motors and sold through Ford dealers, Brewster built its version of the V-8 for a clientele which found it embarrassing to be seen driving anything grander during these depressed years, Ford designer Gregorie came up with a piquant speedster for Edsel, in Europe Alexis Kellner showed some lovely cabriolets. But the production V-8's would come to be viewed in some quarters of the market as not as stylish, not as colorful, not as appealing as the competition.

Nineteen thirty-five had been a good year, however. Ford had passed Chevy, and though this certainly in part was due to an extended strike at the Chevrolet factory, it was attributable also to the new improved line of Ford cars, designated Model 48. Considerably more streamlined, the lines carried unbroken from the slanting radiator grille, along the low hood and up to the sharply angled windshield, the fenders were more highly crowned and deeper, the rear of the car had a smooth flowing contour — and the result led *The New York Times* to note on its editorial page that "Mr. Ford's views on the management of industry may hark back to an older age, but his product keeps pace with the rush of events." Crediting Henry with an industrial influence probably not applicable since his Model T days, the paper concluded, "wind resistance is doomed."

Nearly nine million visitors had crowded Ford showrooms to see the new car, and the various "action" displays demonstrating engine and chassis improvements. The 90 hp V-8 boasted a new system of forced draft crankcase ventilation, the use of aircraft type copper-lead floating connecting rod bearings, a new cast alloy iron camshaft. There was a new clutch, stronger frame and rear axle, and improved brakes "entirely redesigned . . . and especially effective," so *Automotive Industries* reported. But they were still mechanical; Ford salesmen were told that "buyer enlightenment and education" would overcome the mistaken impression that hydraulics were superior. "Center-Poise" ride was the term for the new Ford suspension, devised by moving the engine ahead eight inches so that its weight rested over the front axle, moving the rear seat eight inches forward of the rear axle and attaching longer and more flexible transverse springs four inches forward of the front axle and four inches to the back of the rear axle. This, Murray Fahnestock declared, was tantamount to independent springing of all four wheels. He wasn't terribly convincing.

The late Allan Nevins, De Witt Clinton Professor Emeritus of American History at Columbia University who, with Frank Ernest Hill, authored the estimable three-volume Ford history, suggested that had Ford followed its good year of 1935 with the introduction of a six — the Lincoln Zephyr V-12 had debuted, providing the company in essence with what was a third car, another was needed — and the incorporation of hydraulic brakes, independent front suspension and Hotchkiss drive, that the race for supremacy might have tipped in Ford's favor. But Ford did not, and while Chevrolet (now with hydraulics) and

1936 Model 68 Type 720 Coupe / Owner: Harold Selson

1937 Model 78 Fordor Sedan / Owner: James C. Bru

Plymouth touted their various up-to-date features of comfort and style, the Ford company was left to such comments as "the same design as the brakes that have been used for years on the finest cars in this country and abroad." The argument was wearing thin.

Refinements in the new 1936 Model 68 had reduced steering effort by about twenty-five percent, but it wasn't the "shockless" of the Plymouth nor the "shockproof" of the Chevrolet. Quieter gearshifting was now available with the addition of helical gears in low and reverse, as well as second and high as the previous year. An improved driveshaft to reduce noise at the rear axle and the use of sound deadening material inside were welcome features. New cold-pressed steel wheels were noticeable, as were the more pointed grille, longer hood and deeper fenders. But that wasn't enough. Once again Chevrolet overtook Ford.

Something new was tried for 1937 — two V-8 engines: the venerable 221-cubic-inch unit (since 1936 labeled at 85 hp, though it would occasionally and confusingly be relisted as a 90 hp in later catalogues) and the 136-cubic-inch (2.60 by 3.20 bore and stroke) V-8 of 60 hp (at 3500 rpm) which had been powering French and English Fords for more than a year. The latter, obviously Henry Ford's answer to his dealers' plaints for a six-cylinder car, quelled the many rumors circulating that the company was about to introduce a "baby" Ford and once again moved *The New York Times* to editorialize: "Mr. Ford is always original, and it is just like him to turn out an economy car just when the country is getting rich again and ready to splurge. . . . [But] at 60 hp the American people still have twice as much horsepower as the European nobility uses for its deluxe cars. It is probably twice as much horsepower as we need or is good for us."

The smaller-engined car (Model 74) sold for $529-$664, the larger (Model 78) for $585-$858. Fords had been inching up in price of late. There were some engine refinements and changes — improved cooling, new cast alloy steel pistons, larger "insert" type main bearings — and a new all steel body with one-piece steel top. Streamlining was more pronounced, and Ford had another go at revising the brakes, calling the results "controlled self-energization." The mechanicals now operated through cables in conduits and required about a third less effort than previously. Alas, the "easy action" brakes were found to be too easy acting for some drivers and by year's end the brake linings were changed to a harder type giving less self-energizing and more control. They remained thus for the 1938 line now designated Model 81A De Luxe and Standard (the larger engine) and Model 82A (the 60 hp). There was the same old chassis, but a fresh face and a swept tail, new styling which declining sales figures would indicate was not greeted with overwhelming enthusiasm.

On April 11th, 1938 Henry Ford and his beloved Clara celebrated their golden wedding anniversary. "Pick a good model and stick with it," he told a reporter on that lovely day. "I've been sold on one model for half a century." Henry was nearing his seventy-fifth birthday — and he remained as quotable as ever. But now his newsmaking was taking a decidedly treacherous turn; even his wife, his treasured "Callie," as he called her, would be engulfed by it. And it would devastate his son. Nothing ever would be the same again.

It has long been puzzling to many observers how a man whose social thinking had been so far ahead of his time during one era could fall so far behind it in another. If a simplistic solution is sought, perhaps it need only be said that the times changed but Henry Ford had not. He refused to accept labor's right to organize. Gradually, over the years, things had changed at Ford. From the euphoria of the early $5-a-day era, Ford workers' attitudes came to be neatly summed up in a prayer: "Our Ford who lives in Dearborn, Henry is thy name."

1937 Model 78 Type 770-B Coupe (De Luxe) / Owner: Bob Livingston

With the crush of the Depression, fear and tension had permeated the plants. Discipline was strictly enforced, and led to some almost whimsical measures. In 1931 Ford decreed that every family man in his Iron Mountain plant would be required to grow vegetables — a "shotgun garden," as it was called in the press, and one Ford worker was chastised because he planted pansies around the edge of his. More often whimsy wasn't involved. Holding one's job became a hazard, and the axe fell arbitrarily, striking even Frank Kulick, whose service to Ford went back to Henry's turn of the century racing days. Walter Reuther, a young tool and die maker at Ford, was seated at his bench one day at Highland Park and standing up the next at the Rouge. "You can't work with these fine tolerances standing up," he complained. "You need to be firmly planted." He was fired for union activity. Suspicion of union allegiance would become synonymous with discharge, and company spies would be everywhere. The production line would be speeded up, the workers compelled to keep up — slowing down would mean losing their jobs. Overall factory wages would be reduced by the simple expedient of firing a man from a higher paying job and rehiring him at a lower one.

Behind all this stood the spectre of Harry Bennett, who had been hired as a plant guard during World War I and whose star had risen meteorically after the riot at the Ford plant in 1932 — ten days after the first V-8 had come off the production line — when four men were killed and Harry Bennett, among others, hurt. As an associate remembered, Bennett "had mercurachrome put on his cuts and went to see Ford, and the latter was impressed." That was perhaps minimizing his injuries, but Bennett would not have been the sort to maximize them, except for effect. He was an utterly fearless man, and as picturesque as he was ruthless. Just five inches over five feet tall, he could put to the floor men who towered over him. His relations with the Detroit underworld were entirely open. Director of personnel ostensibly, he was in reality Ford's chief of police, and around him, to enforce the often strong-arm measures common to large industrial plants before unionization, he gathered ex-athletes, ex-detectives and ex-cons — an army some would call the Storm Troops. Charles Sorensen — hardly a diffident personality himself — would later write that these were not "Ford men" and he and Edsel had to continually apologize for their bad manners.

In 1937 the Supreme Court upheld the constitutionality of the Wagner Act, legislated in the wake of FDR's smashing 1936 election victory. Henry couldn't fight both organized labor and the United States government. But he would try. Nearly 5000 strikes swept the nation in 1937, and in their wake industry largely gave in to the fact of unions, both General Motors and Chrysler accepting the validity of the United Auto Workers as a bargaining agent. But not Henry Ford. The Wagner Act compelled collective bargaining, not agreement — and Harry Bennett was sure he could take care of the UAW. Interference, restraint and coercion was the way the National Labor Relations Board would later describe the technique; Bennett was good at it. Henry Ford became very fond of him, looking upon him as a second son almost, his toughness contrasting with what Ford believed was weakness in his own son Edsel. But Henry was wrong.

Edsel begged his father to negotiate a favorable agreement with the union. Henry wouldn't listen. He was listening only to Bennett, and Bennett and Edsel had become mortal enemies. Edsel's inherent decency, his sensitivity, his progressiveness steeled him — but when Edsel tried to convince Henry Ford of the wisdom of his position the father saw the son's strength as recalcitrance. "The hurtful thing about all this," Edsel cried out once, "is that father takes Harry's word . . . and he won't believe mine." Clara Ford saw the matter as even more desperate. "Who is this man," she wept, "who has so much control over my hus-

1937 Model 78 Type 730-D Fordor Sedan (De Luxe Touring) / Jim Showalter

1937 Model 78 Type 750 Phaeton (Touring) / Owner: Ollie Smith

119

1937 Model 78 Town Car by Cunningham / Owner: Frank Schuster

1937 Model 78 Type 720 Coupe (Club) / Owner: L. Martin

1937 Model 78 Type 760-B Cabriolet (Club) / Owner: L. Martin

band and is ruining my son's health?" The situation was doing more than that. It was killing him. The despair, the humiliation, the agony of not being listened to, of watching this great company plunged onto a disastrous course was unbearable.

On May 26th, 1937 came the Battle of the Overpass. At the Rouge plant distributors of union handbills were turned upon by Bennett's army. Selected for particularly brutal beatings were labor organizers Walter Reuther and Richard Frankensteen. Attacked also were reporters and photographers. The entire scene was captured in all its grim horror in newspapers and magazines across the country. In answer to the later NLRB report of what happened that day, Henry Ford said: "Anybody who knows the Ford Motor Company knows that things the Board charged never happened and could not happen here." He simply did not wish to see.

And so he fought on for four years, almost alone, buoyed up for a while by the logistical errors made by the NLRB on the one hand, on the other by the dissension within the UAW. Meanwhile Ford plants were paying workers one to two cents an hour less than the overall national industrial average. And the company's record within the automotive field was even worse. GM and Chrysler men would be over the dollar mark, the men of Ford fractionally over ninety cents. It seemed incredible that this was the company of Henry Ford, the Model T and the $5-day.

Finally it was all over. The Supreme Court declared Ford had violated the Wagner Act. And on April 1st, 1941, it happened spontaneously; with the arbitrary firing of eight union sympathizers, 50,000 men at the Rouge refused to work. Labor organizers hurried over and joined in. Three days later an aroused and determined Edsel convinced his father to negotiate. But when a contract was ready for his signature, Henry refused to sign. Instead he wanted the plant closed down; "I don't want any more of this business," he told Charles Sorensen and Edsel that evening. The next day Sorensen, after hearing on the radio that Ford had agreed to the contract, met with Henry. Henry chatted idly, but said nothing. Edsel came in. Henry talked on for a while, then left the room. "What in the world happened?" Edsel asked. "I was about to ask you the same thing," Sorensen replied. About six weeks later Henry confided that he had spoken to his wife of his plans that evening — and that she had threatened to leave him if he didn't sign. Henry saw it her way. "Don't ever discredit the power of a woman," he advised Sorensen. Good old Henry, how paradoxical, how typical.

Typical, too, was Henry's capitulation. Fighting until fighting was no longer possible, he surrendered by providing the union with even more than it asked, the most favorable contract in the automobile industry. Perhaps he saw that as a personal victory of sorts. General Motors and Chrysler Corporation had come to do more by their workers than he by his. Now he would do them one better. He must have liked that.

Interestingly, and this was probably a reflection of the legend that had become Henry Ford, a *Fortune* poll in 1940 indicated that 75.6 percent of working people believed he had been "helpful to labor," a higher percentage than awarded to Senator Wagner or John L. Lewis. Obviously the mass of America still looked upon the industrialist with favor, even though they were no longer buying his cars in overwhelming numbers (Chevrolet sold nearly 900,000 cars in 1940, Ford 300,-000 less.) The latter didn't concern Henry overly. Though one might doubt his resolve to close down his factory — an ill-considered outburst certainly, even for Henry — one does tend to believe his oft repeated statements that he didn't give a hang what Chevrolet did, or how many cars they built. Figures didn't worry Henry, only his car. If he was pleased with it, he didn't bother about anything

1938 Model 81A Type 730-B De Luxe Fordor Sedan / Owner: Ralph Hubbard

1938 Model 82A Type 770-A Standard Coupe / Owner: Larry Johansen

1939 Model 91A Type 76 De Luxe Convertible Coupe / Henry Ford Museum

1939 Model 91A Type 74 De Luxe Convertible Fordor Sedan / G. Chamberlin

else. He didn't think competitively. "We stopped figuring costs on this one," he said when the V-8 was introduced. He had said about the same for the Model A. Since the book value of Ford of the United States was listed in 1937 as $624,975,000 — no one could compute the exact value of the complex world-wide holdings — Henry could afford to be so single-minded. Or such was his view anyway. He frequently commented that he had too much money.

Very few within the Ford organization shared his sentiments — and by the late Thirties both Edsel and Sorensen agreed that if the company were to survive it would do so, as Allan Nevins has written, despite and not because of Henry Ford. The production engineering quarters were moved away from him shortly thereafter, from Dearborn to the Rouge in early 1937.

The lack of diversification in the company's product line was really hurting now. For 1938 a shorter and narrower model using the smaller V-8 engine was proposed, and a prototype built, but the price differential between it and the other V-8's would have been too slim, and both Henry and Edsel agreed that it shouldn't be produced. For 1939, however, there was a new car; it was called Mercury and was priced between the Ford De Luxe and the Lincoln Zephyr.

The advent of the Mercury probably stole some of the thunder from Ford's switch to hydraulic brakes that year, but the "at last" factor of the latter would no doubt have dictated they be treated with benign neglect anyway. No trumpet fanfare accompanied their introduction, Ford preferring to emphasize instead the fresh styling treatment of the De Luxe models: deep hood, low radiator grille, headlamps flush with fenders. The standard model resembled the De Luxe model of the preceding year, this hand-me-down styling policy having been inaugurated in 1938. The larger V-8's were called Model 91A, the 60 hp variety 922A.

On April 8th, 1940 the 28,000,000th Ford was built. It was viewed in Washington by FDR and Vice President Garner, exhibited at the New York World's Fair and given a tour of the United States, Canada and Mexico. Nearly 600,000 cars like it were sold that year. The 60 hp (now Model 022A) which had never really caught on, still didn't; indeed motoring journals of the period reported that it had been eliminated from the line, though that wasn't true. The larger V-8's were now called Model 01A. New to the cars were a finger-tip gearshift mounted on the steering column, sealed beam headlamps, improvements in braking and suspension, more interior room — and of course the now perennial revised styling treatment for fenders, hood and radiator. A new motorcar from the company, called the Lincoln Continental, also made rather big news this year.

About the time the Mercury was introduced — so the story goes — Edsel had taken it upon himself to promise some of his clamoring dealers that Ford would produce a six. His father happened by about then — and in one of those turnabouts that had practically become his stock in trade, said, "Go ahead, you're the boss." Apparently Edsel recovered his composure quickly enough to get work started — and the result was introduced in 1941 as the Special, replacing the unlamented 60 hp V-8. Henry hadn't anything to do with the engine of this new car (a 3.3 by 4.4 L-head of 226 cubic inches for 90 hp at 3300 rpm), but it would appear he might have had a say in at least one area: the Special was available in any color as long as it was black. "A Ford Six, At Last" headlined *Business Week*. Henry preferred his V-8, now on a 114-inch wheelbase and completely restyled. The Model 11A — now hyperbolized into De Luxe and Super De Luxe — was longer, lower, larger and wider, and as Ford brochures enthused, "the running boards have almost disappeared."

The running boards were done away with altogether for '42, which was all to

1939 Model 91A De Luxe Type 79 Station Wagon / Owner: Dan Krehbiel

1939 Model 91A Type 70-A Standard Tudor Sedan / Owner: Jay Harris

1940 Model 01A Type 78 De Luxe Sedan Delivery / Owner: Tom Burden

1940 Model 01A Type 66 De Luxe Convertible Club Coupe / Owner: Walter H. Up

the good, and the front design took on an overbearing look, which was not. In introducing the car Ford's new (since 1940) advertising agency, McCann Erickson, had allowed that "for these unusual times, Ford Dealers offer an unusual new car." That was the first week of October 1941. Two months later it hardly mattered.

Even when Germany had occupied the Sudetenland in September of 1938, Henry Ford had disallowed the possibility of war. When it came he was equally as vigorous in promoting the cause of America's non-participation in it. With Charles Lindbergh he and Clara were members of the America First committee. He refused to build Rolls-Royce engines for England — and in February of 1941 suggested aid to both Allies and Axis as a solution whereby both sides would exhaust themselves and America could thereafter "help them both make a just peace." Such ideas led to charges that Henry Ford was pro-Nazi. They simply weren't true. "Anything that breeds hate is repulsive to me," he had said. But he also hated the idea of America going to war. Playing on this — and the charges that furled around Ford — Nazi propaganda minister Joseph Goebbels had distributed throughout the Netherlands' provincial press the news that President Roosevelt had ordered the arrest of Henry Ford for "starting the German 'V' for victory campaign by constructing the Ford V-8" and that "English car owners sacrificed their Sunday's rest on July 20th . . . [and] spent the day grinding away the 'V' signs on their Ford V-8's." The absurdity of it is almost beyond comprehension. But how dangerous the Big Lie could be.

Although Sorensen and Edsel were devoted proponents of aiding the international war effort, Henry Ford was enthusiastic for military production only so long as it was geared for American defense purposes. Before Pearl Harbor his company had committed itself to aircraft engine manufacture, was building reconnaissance cars, designing a swamp buggy, involved with the jeep, the M-4 tank, the M-7 Anti-Aircraft Gun Director — and turning the wooded and bucolic setting surrounding a lazy little creek west of Detroit into a project incredibly more formidable than its gentle name would imply. Willow Run would become America's leading producer of heavy bombers: 8686 Liberators. With the attack on Hawaii, weeks before the new War Production Board would order it, Henry Ford called in his executives. "We might as well quit making cars now," he said, and driving around his domain, he pointed to each building, "Get a defense job going in there quick." And so it would be.

The burdens of military production fell heavily on the shoulders of Edsel and Sorensen, and the work was fearsome. Complicating it was also the continuing deteriorating relationship between Edsel and Henry Ford, aggravated by the labor crisis, aided by Harry Bennett's ruthless efforts to hold Edsel in check, abetted by the antagonism Henry began showing towards Edsel's two older sons. During the waning days of the Model T, when Edsel had become too insistent on its replacement, Henry had, in a fit of pique, ordered him to California. Now he suggested the same for Henry II and Benson, who had recently joined the Ford work force. In neither case was the order carried out. Henry was calmed, and the boys remained at the Rouge plant until joining military service.

Finally it was all too much for Edsel. Long in precarious health with stomach ulcers, he gave way to cancer and undulant fever, the latter from drinking the non-pasteurized milk of the Ford farm. On May 26th, 1943 he died of these ailments and, as Allan Nevins has written, a broken heart. He was forty-nine. At the funeral Henry Ford stood tight-lipped in grief. Sorensen broke down. Harry Bennett displayed rare good taste and did not attend. The much loved Edsel was mourned deeply. *The New York Times* said, "the nation has suffered a serious

1940 Model 01A Type 77-A Standard Coupe / Owner: Gordon Chamberlin

1940 Model 01A Type 77-B De Luxe Coupe / Owner: Roger Hudson

loss" — and it wasn't empty rhetoric, for as the advancing years had hardened the father, the son had become the conscience of the company, and a champion of the ideals and progressivism of Henry's own youth.

His death left a gaping void — and a number of questions. The Ford empire had long been split into two factions, Bennett on the one side, Sorensen on the other, with Edsel siding often with the latter as countermeasure to the pervasive influence the former held over Henry Ford. What would happen now? And what of the presidency of the Ford Motor Company itself? As *Time* magazine said, "there seemed to be only one man who could fill it." And on July 30th he would be eighty years old.

Henry Ford took the job anyway. In 1938 he had suffered his first stroke, in 1941 a second one. *Time* wondered tactlessly if the Ford company could "stand the shock of another death," noting that Henry was already eighteen years to the senior of the average U.S. life expectancy. It was Henry, of course, who was primarily responsible for the administrative chaos in which the company lay. After his second stroke, matters had become even worse. Henry played havoc with any plans for organization; John Gunther wrote about this time that "for a generation he carried a billion dollar business under his hat." In 1945 a young man charged with the task of preparing an organization chart gave up in tears "because there was no way of knowing who reported to whom."

Into this quagmire Henry Ford II returned, released from the Navy for, among other reasons, the government's concern with Ford's war production. It was hoped the intense young twenty-five-year-old might be able to straighten matters out. He plunged in — and impressed everyone. "Can you believe it?" Henry II later exclaimed to a reporter. "In one department they figured their costs by *weighing* the piles of invoices on a scale." Somehow he remained undaunted. And he worked incredibly hard.

Early in 1944 Sorensen resigned, probably at the pleasure of Henry Ford. Some time later he wrote that he had been asked by Washington to take over the company for the government — under wartime conditions this could have happened — but he refused, confident that Henry Ford II could handle what war work remained. During the last month of the year previous, the younger Henry had been elected a vice-president, and the ultimate fate of the Ford Motor Company was recognized for those with eyes to see that summer day two years later when Henry II himself announced the facelifted Ford models for 1946. He had the confidence of his grandmother, his mother and his associates in the Ford organization — and on September 21st, 1945 he had the presidency of the Ford Motor Company. It had taken a threat to sell her stock by Mrs. Edsel Ford to do it, but Henry had agreed to step aside and allow his grandson a free hand. One of Henry II's first exercises of authority was to see to the departure of Harry Bennett. It happened that same day. Bennett walked out the door; four months later a group that would become known as the Whiz Kids walked in, followed closely by Ernie Breech — and a new beginning for the company born of one man's vision a half century earlier.

It would be easy to heap abuses upon the Henry Ford of these years, when his mind was crippled and his judgment clouded by strokes. He was a broken old man now — with the measure of his achievements far behind him. "Life," he had commented once, "is work, and when work is over, there is nothing to do but wait for death to take you away." On April 7th, 1947, it did. "The Father of the Automobile Dies" headlined *Life* magazine. And, notwithstanding the qualification with which one must temper such a tribute, in a very real sense he was. No one should ever forget that.

1941 Model 11A Type 77-B Super De Luxe Coupe, this car a pre-production model displayed at a dealer's showing / Owner: John Ryan

SUBJECT AND ILLUSTRATION INDEXES

PHOTOGRAPHY CREDITS

16-17, 18, 19, 20-21, 22-23, 24, 25, 29, 30-31, 34, 35, 36, 42, 49, 54, 57, 68-69, 100 above, 110 above, 124 above: Photographs by Carl Malotka and Charles Miller. 26, 41, 43, 44, 45, 46, 50, 51, 55 above, 60 above, 61, 72 above, 73, 87 above: Photographs by Henry Austin Clark, Jr. 32-33, 113 below left: Photographs by Don Vorderman. 52-53, 55 below, 58, 59, 62, 83 above and below, 107 above: Photographs by L. Scott Bailey. 67, 70, 71, 72 below, 74, 75, 76-77, 78, 79, 81, 82, 84, 85, 86, 87 below, 88, 89, 90, 91, 92-93, 95, 96-97, 100 below, 101, 102, 103, 104-105, 106, 107 below, 108-109, 110 below, 111, 113 above left and right and below right, 114, 115, 116-117, 118, 119, 120, 121, 122, 123, 124 below, 125, 126, 127, 130, 131: Photographs by Rick Lenz. 128-129: Photograph by Stan Grayson. The Henry Ford portraits introducing the various sections of the book are from the following collections: on the title page (Henry, shown with his Model T), 13, 39 and 99 (Henry pictured with Edsel), courtesy of the Ford Archives, Henry Ford Museum; page 65, courtesy of the National Automotive History Collection, Detroit Public Library.

ILLUSTRATION INDEX

The Illustration Index is arranged by era, chronologically within the era, and alphabetically by body style within the chronology. Designations are given as they were written in the Ford literature of the period. This, the reader will note, results in a certain inconstancy. Indeed, for some model years, the designation for the same car appeared in varying guises often within the same brochure. The designations as noted in such cases are the most commonly used throughout the body of the Ford literature of the period for the vehicle involved.